WREATHS
Around the House

WREATHS

Around the House

❧

More Than 80
Distinctive Wreaths to Make,
Enjoy & Give as Gifts

**DEBORAH
MORGENTHAL**

Sterling Publishing Co., Inc.   New York
A STERLING/LARK BOOK

Design: Dana Irwin
Production: Elaine Thompson
Photography: Evan Bracken
Cover Design: Dana Irwin

Library of Congress Cataloguing-in-Publication Data
Morgenthal, Deborah, 1950–
    Wreaths around the house : more than 80 distinctive wreaths to
make, enjoy & give as gifts / Deborah Morgenthal.
       p.   cm.
    "A Sterling/Lark book."
    Includes index.
    ISBN 0-8069-0712-6
    1. Wreaths.   I. Title
TT899.75.M67   1993
745.54'1–dc20   93-39715
                                  CIP

10 9 8 7 6 5 4 3 2 1

A Sterling/Lark Book

First paperback edition published in 1995 by
Sterling Publishing Company, Inc.
387 Park Avenue South, New York, N.Y. 10016

Produced by Altamont Press, Inc.
50 College Street, Asheville, NC 28801

© 1994 by Altamont Press

Distributed in Canada by Sterling Publishing
   % Canadian Manda Group, One Atlantic Avenue, Suite 105
   Toronto, Ontario, Canada M6K 3E7
Distributed in Great Britain and Europe by Cassell PLC
   Wellington House, 125 Strand, London WC2R 0BB, England
Distributed in Australia by Capricorn Link (Australia) Pty Ltd.
   P.O. Box 6651, Baulkham Hills, Business Centre, NSW 2153, Australia

Every effort has been made to ensure that all the information in this
book is accurate. However, due to differing conditions, tools, and
individual skills, the publisher cannot be responsible for any injuries,
losses, and other damages which may result from the use of the information
in this book.

Printed in Hong Kong

Sterling ISBN 0-8069-0712-6 Trade
              0-8069-0713-4 Paper

CONTENTS

INTRODUCTION

Designers of wreaths are on an exciting, creative journey. On this journey they are exploring every aspect of wreath making: times of year and occasions for which wreaths are made; shapes, sizes, and types of bases used; how texture, color, and height affect design; the extraordinary variety and high quality of materials available; and the placement of the wreaths themselves.

Certainly, designers continue to create wreaths specifically as front-door greeters and to usher in the holidays. But there's change here, too. Although some holiday wreaths are festooned with evergreens and red berries, others festively don nontraditional colors and materials. (See page 53.)

In this book you'll find that wreaths are welcome in many rooms throughout the home. Wreaths can be distinctive and decorative accents for many different styles of kitchens, living rooms, dining rooms, sunrooms, bedrooms, baths, and porches. We enjoyed decorating the homes in this book with wreaths. Although we hung most of them on walls, we couldn't resist arranging some in unexpected places: draped around a lamp, propped on a bed, looped around drawer knobs, swooped over mirrors, or nestled in bookshelves.

In addition to what rooms they're in and where they are placed, the wreaths vary enormously in terms of the materials used. You'll find a veritable potpourri

of dried herbs; flowers that are dried, fresh and silk; latex fruits and vegetables; bamboo, lotus pods, and eucalyptus sprayed gold; twigs with fungus and vines with feathers; terra cotta finishes and terra cotta pots; clay cherubs, mushroom birds, neon fish, plush bears—even a miniature rocking chair! And ribbons! Cotton, satin, organdy, mesh, French, and tapestry are here in a splendid array of colors and patterns.

■

Some designers created wreaths using matching fabrics, colors, and details that match the rooms they grace. (See page 48.) Others use the room setting to guide the style of the wreath. And what a range of styles there is: elegant, rustic, whimsical, masculine, dramatic, romantic, tranquil, and festive.

When we contacted designers to help us put this book together, we encouraged them to view the theme of Wreaths Around the House as a no-holds-barred invitation to be creative. We think they came up with some terrific designs, and we hope they inspire you to try your hand at wreath making or to expand your own designs.

■

Some of the wreaths in the book look more complicated than they are. Give them a whirl. You may be surprised at how easy wreath making really is. You may, in fact, find it impossible to duplicate a wreath from this book without changing, rearranging, adding a little more of this or that. What you'll be adding is a very special ingredient—your own creativity!

BASES -
WHERE IT ALL BEGINS

The first decision you'll need to make is what type of base to choose. You'll be guided in this process by the vision of your completed wreath. Each wreath idea is best suited to a particular type of base. The most commonly used bases in this book are vine, straw, and wire, followed by moss-covered bases and foam. Other bases in this book were shaped from plywood.

Bases are available in many different shapes and sizes. Making your own is rewarding too.

Don't overlook found objects: How about a clock, a felt hat, a hula hoop, or a straw plate?

The role the base plays in your wreath will help you select one. If you plan to cover the entire base with flowers, fabric, or shells, then look for an inexpen-

sive base, such as foam, which is available rein-forced with wire to accommodate heavy items.

On the other hand, if the base will be an important decorative element of your wreath, then select a base that can rise to the occasion, such as vine, straw, or moss. (See page 54.)

FOAM

Foam bases are inexpensive and can be found in many stores in white, gray, and green. Although different sizes are available, the broadest range of sizes and shapes come only in white. You can change the color and surface texture by wrapping a white foam base in ribbon or by covering the entire surface with moss or leaves. Covering the base also prevents hot glue from melting the foam. (See page 97.)

More creative base options can be found, such as foam bases with mirrors in the center, foam bases covered with grated cinnamon, and bases made from floral foam to lengthen the life of fresh flow-ers. Or you can purchase sheets of Styrofoam and cut or bend the material into the shape you desire.

You can also find larger foam bases that come with a thick wire ring molded into the foam to make the base stronger. This is important if your design includes heavy items, or if the materials will be arranged unevenly around the base.

VINES

Vines are one of the most widely used bases. Their popularity is related to several factors. Vines comple-ment many different wreath designs; they can be an integral design element of the wreath itself, either in their natural color or painted (see page 88)); they can be fashioned into a variety of shapes and sizes; they are sturdy enough to support heavy items; and lastly, they give the wreath a very "natural" look.

STRAW

Straw is another popular base material that is readily available in stores. It's easy to attach materials directly onto the sturdy base using floral picks, wire, or hot glue. It's especially reliable if you'll be attaching heavy items. (See page 96.) You can also alter the look by covering a straw base with moss or ribbon.

Another advantage of a straw base is that you can take a round one and reshape it into an oval or a square. Stores now carry heart shapes, as well. Straw bases are hearty and forgiving, although somewhat bulky. They, too, can provide just the right contrast in color or texture you're looking for.

MOSS

Wreath makers like moss bases for a number of reasons. To begin with, it's easy to glue items onto their surface, to pick in flowers with floral picks, and to insert single stems of flowers or greenery. Also, the base itself can be an attractive part of the wreath and doesn't need to be completely covered by decorative materials. (See page 42.)

Moss bases can be found in craft stores and come in different sizes. Or, you can cover a foam or straw base with moss to create a surface that's more receptive to hot glue. Arrange the moss around the top and sides of the base, and glue it on or secure it in place with floral pins or thin-gauge floral wire. Popular mosses include Spanish, sheet, and reindeer. (If you use moss you've gathered yourself, be sure to microwave it for a few minutes to rid your wreath of any nesting insects.)

WIRE

Wire bases can be purchased in craft stores and come in a variety of sizes, in both single or concentric rings. Double-wire ring forms allow you to create a flat, wide surface by wrapping ribbon or paper around the two rings. This makes a receptive surface onto which you can glue large, delicate items that would break if you tried to fold them around the curves of other types of bases.

Single-wire bases are a nice complement for delicate and light-weight materials such as dried flowers. Large items won't work with these bases because there's so little surface area on which to glue materials. Single wires come crimped, too, a help in wiring on items. One way to work with wire rings for dried wreaths is to cover the frame with bunches of artemisia wound tightly around the base with monofilament. This gives you a broad surface for attaching other flowers, and the artemisia blends in beautifully with the completed wreath. (See page 59.)

Multiple-wire ring forms with wire arranged at different depths are popular because the groove that runs all around the circle can be packed with natural materials or floral foam to provide a soft bed in which your other materials can nest. Fragrant sweet Annie, artemisia, or any type of moss work well. Also called box wreaths, these bases can provide a wide surface for tying or wiring on novelty items. (See page 112.)

MAKING YOUR OWN VINE BASE

Although you can find vine bases in most garden and flower stores, why not try making your own? Search for vines in the fall and spring. Grapevines are the strongest, and honeysuckle and wisteria more delicate and fanciful. Start with freshly cut vine—you'll find it less likely to split when you bend it. If the vines have sat for a while after cutting, you can soak them to make them more pliable.

With long vines, form one piece into a circle somewhat larger than the size base you want to end up with. Then, add more strands of vine until the base is as thick as you'd like. Hold the vine strands together by wrapping the longest vine or a short piece around the other rows. Different looks can be achieved depending on how you twist that final vine around the base. If you're working with shorter vine strands, hold four to six vines together and form a circle. Then, secure them by overlapping a single piece of vine horizontally around the bundle.

Much of the charm of a vine base is the irregularity of the pieces: some have wandering tendrils that add excitement to a wreath like unruly strands of hair. Experiment with the base by adding more vines and winding all of them either in one direction or in alternating directions. Making your own vine base can be a key to the entire design of your wreath.

MAKING YOUR OWN STRAW BASE

Unless you have hay fever, you'll find it fun and easy to make a straw base. Any type of hay, alfalfa, or dried grasses can be fashioned into a base of the size and shape you want.

Start with a handful of straw about one foot (30 cm.) long, and press it tightly, arranging the thickest part in the center and tapering both ends. A thickness of 1-1/2 inches (4 cm.) makes a strong base, but a thinner base may be more appropriate for your wreath design. You'll hold the straw together with floral wire. With your other hand, spiral the straw with wire at intervals of one inch (2.5 cm.), making sure the wire is tight enough to bundle the straw securely.

Continue adding other segments of straw of the same thickness to the base in this way. Now you can begin to curve the finished pieces into the shape and size base you desire. The last step is to overlap the tapered ends and wind wire completely around the base. Trim the wire and, if you like, make a hook that can serve as a way to hang your wreath.

Reinforcing the base with wire can be important if your wreath must support heavy items. You can shape the base out of a coat hanger or other heavy wire. The wire must be large enough to accommodate the thickness of the sides. Follow the instructions above, shaping the straw around the wire.

FILLING A MULTIPLE-WIRE BASE

If you start out with fresh moss or flowers, it's best to let everything dry first so that shrinkage can take place before you fill the base with the materials. Pack the groove with the dried moss or flowers. Then securely wrap the materials with floral wire at intervals of two inches (5 cm.).

MATERIALS
(ALMOST) ANYTHING GOES

DOINGS THINGS NATURALLY

Using wreaths to celebrate and decorate is a time-honored tradition in many cultures, spanning hundreds of centuries. Plants and flowers are as popular a choice today as they were for our wreath ancestors. Wreaths made of leaves were used as prizes during the ancient Greek Olympics. Early Egyptians wore floral wreaths as collars. During the emotionally reserved Victorian era, feelings, especially amorous ones, were expressed in flower-language, with each type of flower conveying a specific meaning.

Symbolism aside, the beauty, fragrance, and infinite variety of nature's gifts will persuade you to include fresh, dried, or preserved flowers, herbs and greenery in your wreath making.

FRESH FLOWERS

If permanence is not a criterion, consider using fresh flowers. Perhaps because their beauty is so fleeting, fresh flowers in a wreath can be gorgeous. To extend their beauty, you can purchase wet foam or moss bases at florist shops. You can also buy small plastic tubes that, attached to your wreath and filled with water, can

offer your flowers a drink for several days. When the flowers wilt, simply replace them with fresh ones.

DRIED FLOWERS

Both beauty and long life can be achieved with dried flowers and herbs, which is why they are so popular with wreath designers. Florists, nurseries, and craft stores carry a wide selection. Or you can dry the ones you're growing in your garden! The color and fragrance of the garden, though somewhat subdued, can be enjoyed for many months.

To ensure a long life for your dried flower wreath, display it out of direct sunlight and in a location where it won't get brushed against. Some flowers, such as German statice and baby's breath, can be picked into a wreath base when fresh and left to dry in place.

EVERGREENS

Nearly everyone can recollect a holiday wreath displayed on a front door. Most likely it was made with fragrant evergreen boughs, shiny pine cones, and a bright red bow. Although evergreens continue to be a staple of

Christmas wreaths, the variety of holiday designs using evergreens is simply astonishing. (See page 32.)

What's more, you don't have to wait until Christmas to enjoy decorating with evergreens. (See page 44.) Year round, you can find fragrant pine, spruce, fir, and hemlock. Other types of evergreen can be used, too. Holly, cedar, boxwood, juniper, cypress, and ivy are all excellent materials. They can serve as the base of your wreath, wired to a straw or wire base, or they can be glued on in smaller pieces as decorative accents.

CONES, NUTS, SEEDS, AND PODS

Yes, you can buy these items in craft stores. But why not make an attentive walk through the woods or a careful tour of your backyard an essential part of the experience? Nature is very thoughtful to wreath design-ers, offering up a seemingly endless supply of attractive materials.

Seed pods and seed heads, cones of all descriptions, fallen birds' nests, lichens and mosses, and gnarled branches are treasures of color, texture, and shape. You can alter the look of these materials with spray paint, porcelain setting agents and high gloss spray.

BERRIES

Don't overlook the simple berry when choosing
design materials. Berries add beauty to many types
of wreaths, not just your basic red-holly-on-green-
bough Christmas variety. You can find berries in
almost as many colors as flowers.

FRUITS AND VEGETABLES

Fresh and dried fruits and vegetables offer wreath
makers a cornucopia of colors, textures and shapes
with which to work. They harmonize beautifully with
flowers, and can be used alone to create a wreath
that is truly a feast for the eyes. You can make appetizing table wreaths as centerpieces using fresh fruits
and vegetables. You can tuck a few bunches of
grapes into a flower wreath. You can even cover a
wreath base with fresh lettuce instead of Spanish
moss. Keep in mind that fresh produce is heavy. Use
hot glue for small items (unless you intend to eat
them!); medium-weight items can be attached with
picks; pins works for large, light-weight materials;
and heavy produce may require wire and glue.

Dried fruits and vegetables are lighter and can give a
wreath a very special look. To dry oranges, lemons
and grapefruits, slice thinly and dry the fruit on a
cookie sheet in a very low oven (about 200°F or 93°C)
for two to three hours, turning the fruit several times
as it dries. Remove the slices before they are brown,
and allow them to completely dry on a drying rack.

RIBBONS AND BOWS

You have many options for enhancing your wreath design and branding it with your personality. Ribbons and bows are the two most frequently used embellishments. A large, flower chintz bow may be the unifying element that transforms your wreath from so-so to outstanding. Try wrapping a wreath with a ribbon or weaving it through vines or greenery to provide color accents. (See page 94.)

The hardest part may be choosing what you want from among all the myriad ribbon choices. Satin, cotton, paper, velvet, French, lace, raffia, and cellophane have distinctive qualities and most come in a variety of colors and patterns.

Roaming through a well-stocked fabric store can be as appetizing (and dangerous!) as a trip to the bakery. Purchase a small sample of different types of ribbon, and try to make bows and other fancies with them. That's the best way to learn about their characteristics.

BEADS, BUTTONS, AND BUNNIES

The appeal of wreaths derives, in large part, from their ability to capture a small slice of nature and life—if only for a short while. This is apparent in the desire of wreath makers to use fresh flowers and collectibles from a walk in the woods or a stroll on the beach. In this way, the wreaths are saying: "Remember This."

Many designers use representational objects that have personal or universal meaning, such as teddy bears for a nursery wreath or a cross on an Easter wreath. (See page 95.)

Next time you clean out the hall closet or restore order to your child's room, don't be so quick to throw things away. That frayed doll's hat, cherished Christmas ornament, shell necklace from Florida, or rhinestone button from grandma's sweater may be perfect for a wreath you haven't even thought about making yet. Store them in your wreath-idea box and wait for inspiration to strike!

FUN WITH FAKES

Even a bee may be fooled. Only a bee will be disappointed. The artificial flowers, fruit, and foliage available today are that convincing. Whether made from silk, latex, or parchment paper, today's variety of artificials accomplishes a dazzling imitation of nature, down to veins on a leaf and the subtle colors of a flower.

If you're ready to walk on the wild side, you also can find fake flowers, foliage, and fruits in colors and sizes not authorized by Mother Nature. Many of the designs in this book combine natural materials, natural looking artificials, and obviously fake ingredients. It's all part of the fun of wreath making.

For certain types of wreaths, artificials offer a number of advantages, starting with their longevity and ease of use. Fake flowers, for instance, have wire stems that make it simple to bend or place them into a wreath base. Moreover, you can take your wreath apart and reuse the materials in other wreaths. Artificials also are easy to clean with a light feather duster or aerosol spray cleaner.

HOW TO DRY FLOWERS AND HERBS

Drying flowers is so simple you'll wonder why you never tried it before! Pick your flowers or herbs when they seem the most lovely to you. Wait until the dew has dried so that the flowers have a head start on drying all the way. Harvest them before midday because hot sun affects the plants' chemistry and lessens their color and fragrance.

You'll want to cut the stems long and remove lower leaves. This makes it easy to tie six to ten stems together with string or yarn and hang them upside down. A dry, dark location is the key to successful drying—a shady corner of a room works fine.

Drying times will vary depending on the type of flower and how much moisture it holds. The average range is four days to two weeks. You'll know they're dry when a stem snaps easily and the flowers feel rigid. Pick a generous bunch of flowers because drying causes them to shrink quite a bit.

ATTACHMENT

ALTERNATIVES AND TIPS

You are well on your way to making a wreath. You've decided on a base and you've collected your decorative materials. Now you need to know what options are available for attaching the items to the base. Attaching is not at all difficult once you gain some experience with a few indispensable tools: wire, picks, tape, pins, and hot glue.

FLORAL WIRE, PICKS, TAPE, AND PINS

Floral wire is flexible wire that is painted green, brown or silver. Plain steel wire works, too, but floral wire blends in with many wreath materials and comes in straight lengths, on spools, or in coils. Floral wire is sold by gauge, or thickness. The higher the gauge, the finer and more flexible the wire.

Wire is the best means of attaching heavy decorations, novelties, large bows, bunches of greenery, and other bulky items. Moreover, you can use wire with almost every type of base. In many cases, however, you'll need to be creative about how you camouflage the wire after you've attached something to the base. Consider gluing on a few dried flower blossoms or plastic berries, or drape a strand of ribbon in a strategic pattern.

Monofilament is popular, too, for some things, such as securing moss or dried flowers to a wire or straw base.

ATTACHING WITH WIRE

The first step is to locate a place on your item where the wire will not be visible. Wrap the wire around the item so that both ends are on its back side. Then twist both ends of the wire tightly together. Hold the object firmly against the wreath base and wrap the wire around the base. With a vine base, you may be able to wrap the wire around a strand of vine. For heavy items, consider reinforcing with hot glue.

If you're wiring a piece of plastic fruit, you may want to insert two wires through the bottom side of the fruit, bend all four ends down, and twist them together. Experiment yourself with the best way to wire your items. The good news about wiring is that if you don't like how it looks on the wreath, or if you don't like its placement, you can easily unwire it and try again.

When you wire flowers to a base, you may want to wire the stems first to prevent delicate flowers from drooping. Place a medium-gauge length of wire next to the stem, and tape the two together using floral tape. Or, you can wrap a fine wire around the stem near the flower head, and then spiral the wire down the stem's length. Either way, you'll want to cover the wire with floral tape. You can even replace an unwieldy stem with a medium-gauge wire by inserting it through the center of the flower and securely hooking the blossom.

FLORAL TAPE

As explained above, floral wire and tape are terrific partners when you need to attach items to a wreath. Although floral tape is not the most adhesive tape available, it does adhere to itself when stretched, and it comes in dark green, light green, and brown, which makes it handy when you want to camouflage a wire.

FLORAL PICKS

These slender pieces of wood will become your best friend when it comes to attaching natural materials to a wreath base. Sharp sticks with thin wires attached at the blunt ends, they are used to secure stems of flowers or foliage that are too weak to insert directly into a foam or straw base. You can pick in a single flower at a time,

or attach small bouquets of materials to a single pick. The picks come in green or natural wood, ranging in length from three to six inches (7.5 cm. to 15 cm.).

Here's how you would "pick" a single spray or a cluster of several small flowers. First, break or cut the plant stems to about half the length of the pick. Then, hold the pick parallel to the stems of the flowers or foliage, with the wired end butting up to the flower heads. Make sure the pointed end is longer than the stems. Starting at the top and spiraling downward, wrap the wire around the stems and the pick itself. If you finish up by wrapping floral tape around the pick and stem, you strengthen that bond and make insertion even easier.

Decorative items other than natural materials or large items such as pine cones can be glued onto the top end of the pick and then picked into the wreath base.

If your base is straw, foam, moss, or certain types of vine, you'll insert the picks into the surface at an angle and continue picking materials in at the same angle around the wreath. You'll need to overlap the materials to hide the picks. The last pick can be inserted under the first. On wire bases or loosely meshed vine bases, hot glue or wire may be required to attach the picks. If the natural materials are particularly heavy, you may want to use hot glue as well.

FLORAL PINS

The last tool that starts with the word "floral" is the simple, U-shaped floral pin, also called a fern or greening pin. These little gems come in very handy when you need to attach moss to a base or secure a small flower or cluster of herbs. They work best when inserted at an angle to the base. You can buy the pins in green or silver to blend in with your materials.

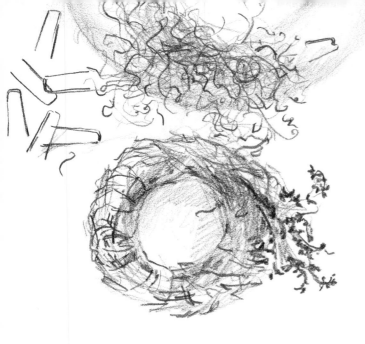

GLUE GUNS AND HOT-MELT GLUE

Last but not least in the wreath making tool department is hot-melt glue, dispensed with a glue gun. Available at discount, hardware, and craft stores, it's available in a standard and mini-size, the latter having a mini-price, too. After you've worked with a glue gun for a short while, you'll wonder how wreath makers in ancient Greece survived without one! Perfect for attaching a single flower blossom or securing a small novelty item in place, the glue forms a nearly invisible and very strong bond.

A glue gun heats and then liquifies opaque sticks of glue that are available in different lengths and are quite inexpensive. A small dollop of the melted glue delivered directly onto the item will do the trick; then, hold the glued item in place for a few seconds to allow it to set. For a heavy item, you may need to wire it to the base first and then reinforce with hot glue. (Any thin strands of dried glue adhering to your wreath can be pulled off when you're finished.)

There are several precautions you'll need to take when working with glue guns, all related to the theme of "hot."

1. A little bit of melted glue inevitably leaks out of the gun even when you're not squeezing the trigger. Be sure to cover your work surface with paper or some other protective material.

2. When plugged in, the tip of the gun gets very hot and could ignite a flammable surface. A glass or ceramic plate placed under the tip solves this potential problem.

3. This stuff is hot! Be attentive when you use it or you may burn your fingers. If this happens a lot, you may be better off purchasing a warm-melt gun that melts glue at a lower temperature.

4. If you're using a foam base, test the surface with a dab of hot glue to see if it melts a hole in it. If it does, you can wrap the base with ribbon, moss, fabric, or other material.

5. Keep glue guns away from the reach of children. They are hot for several minutes, even after they've been unplugged.

PUTTING IT

ALL TOGETHER

There are great cooks who would never think of deviating one garlic bud from the printed recipe. Others add their mark with a little less oregano here, a little more cheese there. Still others won't even look at a recipe. Wreath makers are quite similar. You'll discover your own approach as you go.

For example, you may find that in working with this book, you'll be completely happy following the instructions given for each wreath. But you may feel inclined to substitute a different dried flower, or to insert the eucalyptus stems in alternating angles. That's great! Or, you may take your inspiration from a wreath you see here, close the book, and design your own, unique creation. The choice is entirely yours. That's what makes wreath making so appealing.

The key to a successful design—no matter how intricate or fundamental—is simply this: when the wreath is completed, you should be able to sit back and say, "This looks great!"

Many experienced designers give the following advice: Don't give up halfway through. Keep going and the finished piece may indeed add up to be more, much more, than the sum of the parts.

DESIGNERS

SPEAK OUT

Throughout this book, designers will share with you, in their own words, their observations about color, texture, line, shape, size, and choice of materials. We hope their experience and their work invite you to begin or to expand your own exciting journey with wreath making. The following tips will serve you well no matter what style of wreath design you favor.

ATTACHING

Think of putting on the heaviest items first since they may require wiring that you'll want to camouflage later with smaller things. Attach the most delicate items last to prevent damaging them.

FOCAL POINT

Often, the focal point of the wreath is attached first, usually because it's the largest. Your wreath's focal point might be a plump bow, a painted bird, or a cluster of dried roses.

ANGLE

The angle at which you attach your items will create very different looks. Try applying them all at the same angle, and you'll create a spiral effect. Or, use different angles in different areas.

SECTIONING

Your wreath can be divided up into several distinct areas and treated differently. For instance, you can start with the inner area around the hole and decorate it first, then move to the outer circle, and finish off with the face of the wreath. Or you can imagine your wreath has four quarters, and use these to balance the wreath design or to effect an asymmetrical appearance.

COLOR

Even designers who favor all natural materials enjoy using spray paint to add tinges of color to flowers, pine cones, or vine bases. Craft stores carry a fantastic array of spray paint colors with which you can experiment.

HEIGHT

Wreaths can have height, meaning the appearance of three-dimensions. This is achieved by using flowers or materials of varying heights so that some come out of the wreath towards you, while others lie flat.

"AN INTERESTING THING YOU
CAN DO WITH A VINE BASE IS TO
UNWRAP SOME OF THE VINES AND
PULL THEM OUT TO CREATE
A WIDER BASE. IF YOU ATTACH
MATERIALS TO THESE VINES, YOU CAN CREATE
APPEALING DESIGNS AND GIVE THE EYE A
REASON TO TRAVEL FROM THE TOP OF THE
WREATH TO THE BOTTOM."

—LUCK MCELREATH

"WHEN WORKING WITH A STRAW BASE, IT REALLY IS BETTER
TO LEAVE THE PLASTIC WRAP ON. PICKS GO IN MUCH
EASIER. IF YOU'RE USING SILK OR DRIED FLOWERS,
YOU CAN FILL IN AROUND THEM WITH FOLIAGE OR MOSS
TO COMPLETELY COVER THE PLASTIC.

—NORA BLOSE

DOOR

FEW HOMES CELEBRATE CHRISTMAS
AS BEAUTIFULLY AND ON SUCH A GRAND SCALE
AS BILTMORE HOUSE, THE LARGEST PRIVATE HOME
IN AMERICA, LOCATED IN ASHEVILLE, NORTH
CAROLINA. DURING "CHRISTMAS AT BILTMORE,"
AN ON-GOING FESTIVAL IN NOVEMBER AND
DECEMBER, MANY GORGEOUS WREATHS AND OTHER
FLORAL ARRANGEMENTS ARE ON DISPLAY IN THE
60 ROOMS OPEN TO THE PUBLIC. THIS LARGE AND
MAGNIFICENT WREATH IN SUBDUED REDS AND
GREENS MAKES A LARGE SCALE IMPRESSION
ON BILTMORE HOUSE VISITORS.

START WITH a 36-inch (91.4 cm.) artificial evergreen wreath. Wire together clusters of each
type of dried flower and greenery and pick the
clusters into the base, using glue where necessary to reinforce. You'll need: cockscomb, glycerine-preserved gilded holly leaves and maiden-
hair fern, pennyroyal, rattail statice, Ti tree,
globe amaranth, red bottlebrush, salal leaves,
pink pepperberries, and two or three banksia.
Pick in glycerine-preserved cedar and boxwood.
Build the wreath up so that the sides and edges
are full and three-dimensional. To lighten the
wreath, tuck in sheep's head hydrangea amidst
the other flowers. Lastly, wire on a tapestry
bow. (This wreath can be made on a smaller
scale for your own front door.)

In certain lights, this handsome teasel wreath looks like it's made of feathers, which is ironic because one touch tells you it's prickly, not downy. (The other magic thing about this wreath is what happens when you add a red or green bow.)

Be very careful working with teasel. You may want to use sandpaper to remove the briars on the stems. Start with a straw base wrapped in green plastic. Brush the teasel heads lightly if small particles are caught in the texture. Spray each head with silver paint, and then hold the teasel upright and spray again to cover the little indentations. Pick the teasel heads. Working from the top of the wreath, insert the teasel into the base. (Long-nose pliers work great for grasping the pick and stem and helping to push the teasel into the base.) Position the teasel heads so they point down each side of wreath. Allow a space at the top for a bow. Make a full bow and wire it on. Finally, spray the Queen Anne's lace and glue it into place.

THIS TWIG WREATH, WITH ITS BOLD LINES, VIBRANT COLORS AND BRIGHT-EYED OWLS, EVOKES THE SUNNY DAYS OF AUTUMN WE ALL CHERISH. (WE WERE SO BOLD AS TO HANG IT ON THE LOWER HALF OF THE DOOR.)

START WITH a 20-inch (51 cm.) twig base and wire on a styrofoam block. Using floral picks to attach the materials, create your harvest cornucopia in the following order: birch twigs; artificial anemones, orange and red flowers, and heather; dried Billy balls, rye (dyed red), and cattail; Spanish moss with nesting owls (made from mushrooms); oak leaves, and plastic fruit.

"WREATHS THAT HAVE A CONTEMPORARY LOOK USUALLY ZOOM IN ON ONE FOCAL AREA AND THEN EVERYTHING ELSE BUILDS ON THAT. THIS IS IN CONTRAST TO A WREATH WHERE MATERIALS ARE EQUALLY DISTRIBUTED ALL AROUND THE BASE."

—TOMMY WALLEN

THE BIRCH BARK IN
THIS STUNNING HOLIDAY
WREATH TRANSPORTS
THE CRISP, WINTER
FOREST RIGHT TO
YOUR FRONT DOOR.

START WITH a Spanish moss-covered straw wreath or add the moss yourself. Open up a vine wreath and unwind enough strands to encircle the straw wreath and to extend to the top. Cluster pieces of artificial cedar on picks and insert into the base, making sure they all angle in the same direction. Attach the pine cones using picks and wire. Entwine ribbon around the wreath and secure it in various places with greening pins. Glue on the pomegranates. Attach berry clusters to picks and insert into the base. Glue on assorted pieces of birch bark, clusters of German statice, and reindeer moss. To add an authentic forest scent, pick in pieces of fresh Fraser fir.

"BEING FAMILIAR WITH THE MECHANICS OF ASSEMBLING A WREATH CAN SAVE TIME AND EFFORT. THERE ARE SEVERAL WAYS TO ATTACH MATERIALS TO A WREATH BASE. EXPERIMENT AND LEARN WHAT WORKS BEST WITH DIFFERENT MATERIALS AND ON DIFFERENT BASES."

—JULIANNE BRONDER

Here's a partridge in a pear tree sure to lend a merry welcome to family and friends at Christmas and throughout the year.

Start by removing the plastic wrap from a straw wreath. Spray the entire wreath with glossy wood-tone spray paint to tone down the straw color. Wrap strands of vine around the upper half of the wreath to create a branch effect. Insert artificial pear branches to establish a tree shape, and secure the fruit with floral picks and hot glue. Add green sheet moss to the bottom half of the wreath, and fill in the rest of the wreath with other mosses and lichens, securing them with floral pins and glue. Place the partridge in the bed of mosses. Lastly, pick in the ribbon loops, allowing the streamers to wind through the foliage.

FOYER

THE LIGHT-FILLED STAIRCASE PROVIDES A SIMPLE AND ELEGANT BACKDROP FOR THE VARIED COLORS AND TEXTURES OF THIS WREATH.

USE HOT GLUE to attach the artificial apples, grapes and tomatoes to a 14-inch (35.6 cm.) grapevine wreath. Glue on the dried pine tree greenery next. Add other dried flowers, including yarrow, hydrangea, pepper-berries, and statice. Glue on the bittersweet twigs, and then fashion your silk ribbon bow and wire it to the wreath base.

"PEOPLE ARE INTIMIDATED BY THE COST OF MATERIALS. YOU DON'T HAVE TO SPEND A FORTUNE ON MAKING A WREATH. DECIDE HOW MUCH YOU WANT TO SPEND, AND SPEND MOST OF IT ON HIGH QUALITY MATERIALS THAT WILL BE THE 'STAR' OR THE FOCAL POINT OF THE WREATH. THEN ADD TO IT WITH LESS EXPENSIVE THINGS OR WITH WHAT YOU ALREADY HAVE AT HOME OR IN YOUR BACKYARD."
—LUCK MCELREATH

THE BUTTERY YELLOW WALLS PROVIDE A SUNNY BACKGROUND FOR THIS CHEERFUL
AND WELCOMING DRIED SUNFLOWER WREATH.

START WITH a 10-inch (25.4 cm.) straw wreath and reinforce it with floral wire. The wreath takes its shape from the bracken ferns that are inserted using floral picks. Position the ferns so that they angle out of the wreath instead of lying flat. Insert the larkspur in varying heights, following a spiral design. Pick in the sunflowers with the aim of creating loose, asymmetrical clusters. Then pick in the other dried flowers in this order: sandfordi, sweet Annie, rye, and lemon leaf. Use Spanish moss to cover any picks that may show.

THIS STUNNING DRIED
FLOWER WREATH WOULD
MAKE A TERRIFIC FIRST
IMPRESSION IN
YOUR HOME.

USING GREENING PINS,
attach green oak leaves
to a 16-inch (40.5 cm.)
straw base that is cov-
ered in green plastic.
Cluster green sweet
Annie on floral picks
four to five inches in
length (10 cm. - 12.5
cm.) and insert them
into the base. Add
bundles of Ti tree
(dyed pink) in the
same manner. Pick in
or glue on white and
pink larkspur. For the
lacy finishing touch,
glue on the caspia.

THIS WREATH PAYS
TRIBUTE TO
THE ERA IN ANCIENT
GREECE WHEN LAUREL
WREATHS WERE AWARDED
TO ATHLETES OF
OUTSTANDING ABILITY.
WE LIKED ITS CLASSIC
SIMPLICITY.

GLUE ARTIFICIAL
LEAVES to a molded
Styrofoam wreath
form by applying
hot-melt glue to
the lower third of
each leaf on its
back side and
quickly pressing
the leaf to the
base. To achieve
the "crest" effect,
apply the leaves
individually, begin-
ning at the top of the
wreath and orienting
them in opposite direc-
tions so that the tips
meet at the apex of the
wreath. Glue on the
next tier of leaves so
that about one-third
overlap the first level.
Continue in this man-
ner until you've covered
half of the wreath on
each side. Bind the
wreath with gold cord-
ing where the opposite
sides meet.

"TO ME LINE IS VERY IMPORTANT IN WREATH MAKING. IT'S WHAT
GIVES THE WREATH IT'S DISTINCT STYLE. I WORK WITH THE
ENTIRE WREATH, USING EACH MATERIAL ONE A TIME,
RATHER THAN LOOKING AT THE WREATH IN SECTIONS."
—JAMIE McCABE

THIS STRIKING WREATH
HAS A HIDDEN SECRET:
THE DESIGNER
DELIBERATELY
PURCHASED INEXPENSIVE
ARTIFICIAL FLOWERS
FROM A DISCOUNT STORE
TO DEMONSTRATE THAT
BEAUTY DOESN'T HAVE
TO BREAK THE BANK.

START WITH a 14-inch
(35.6 cm.) grapevine
wreath. Cut out two
three-inch (7.6 cm.)
blocks of floral foam
and glue them to the top
and bottom of the base.
(The other secret to this
wreath is the way the
unwrapped vine leads
your eye to travel from
top to bottom.) Unwrap
the outer strands so they
stand away from the rest
of the base, and glue
on the purple statice.
Create two bouquets for
the top and bottom,
using artificial daffodils,
African violets, roses, ivy,
pansies, Liatris, assorted
pink and yellow flowers,
philodendron and ivy.
Pick the flowers and
foliage into the floral
foam, and glue on the
moss to cover the foam.

THE MAGNIFICENCE OF THIS WREATH COMES FROM ITS SIZE, THE MORE THAN 20 VARIETIES OF DRIED FLOWERS AND HERBS USED, AND ITS POSITIONING UNDERNEATH AN ENORMOUS WROUGHT-IRON CHANDELIER SIX FEET IN DIAMETER. THE WREATH IS ON DISPLAY AT DEERPARK RESTAURANT ON BILTMORE ESTATE. SCALE THE WREATH BACK TO FIT UNDER A CHANDELIER IN YOUR FOYER OR DINING ROOM, AND YOU'LL BE BRINGING HOME A HINT OF GRANDEUR.

UNDERNEATH all those flowers is a 36-inch (91.4 cm.) straw base. Create bunches of the various dried herbs, dried and silk flowers, and dried and artificial fruit, and pick them into the base. Included in the wreath are dried bracken fern, artemisia, tansy, yarrow, lavender, cockscomb, sandfordi, sunflowers, banksia, nigella, orientalis, acroclinium, pomegranates, chili peppers, and wild grasses. The artificial materials include cranberries, violets, crepe myrtle, rubberized greenery, and a selection of pink flowers.

"I TAKE TIME SELECTING MY MATERIALS—A PLEASING COMBINATION TAKES PLANNING. YOU CAN GET GOOD IDEAS FROM LOOKING AT WREATH BOOKS AND FROM STUDYING MATERIALS IN CRAFT AND FLORAL STORES."

—JULIANNE BRONDER

LIVING ROOM

T HIS GORGEOUS DOUBLE WREATH,
DESIGNED WITH AN UNUSUAL MEDLEY OF
NATURAL AND ARTIFICIAL INGREDIENTS,
WILL DEFINITELY BE THE CENTER
OF ATTENTION NO MATTER
WHERE IT'S DISPLAYED.

WIRE TWO VINE BASES together. Unravel a few
of the outer strands so they can encircle
both wreaths. Cover the vine bases with
sheet moss. Glue on the cornucopia of
flowers, fruits, and foliage: silk variegated
ivy, latex day lilies and poppies, silk rose
clusters, blue silk flowers, small silk artichokes, dried sarracenia lilies, and artificial
blackberries. Lastly, weave a French ribbon
through the wreath.

THIS SUMMERY
WREATH BRINGS
INDOORS A VERDIGRIS-
COLORED GARDEN,
BUT THE WREATH
BEGAN ITS LIFE AT
CHRISTMAS. THE
DESIGNER REMOVED
THE HOLIDAY
ORNAMENTS, DRIED IT
OUTSIDE, AND THEN
TRANSFORMED IT
COMPLETELY WITH
NEW ELEMENTS.

START WITH a large, live greenery wreath that has dried thoroughly. Spray the wreath with smokey green floral paint. Spray some assorted dried greenery and glue it to the base. Tie each of the six dried yellow roses with a bow fashioned from the pink satin ribbon. Glue onto the wreath. Then glue on several rose petals so that they appear to have been blown by the wind. For added fullness, glue on six silk flowers at the bottom.

Elegance and grace describe this dried flower wreath, thanks to shades of pink and blue and the frilly lace of white larkspur. Dogwood blossoms and ferns add a hint of the mountains, and the dried herbs make this wreath as pleasing to the nose as to the eyes.

Cover a 12-inch (30.5 cm.) Sweet Huck twig wreath with bracken fern of varying heights, using hot glue to secure. Following a spiral design, glue on the other flowers in this order: blue globe thistle, white larkspur, mint, oregano, sweet Annie, dusty miller, and rattail statice. Carefully glue on the fragile and expensive roses, dogwood, and hydrangea. Use Spanish moss last to add fullness.

"The most interesting wreaths to me are those that have what I call 'ins and outs,' meaning that the flowers and foliage are of varying heights which result in a design that entices your eye to travel in and out of the wreath. This gives the wreath depth and the visual interest of being more three-dimensional."

—Cathy Barnhardt

"I FIND IT EXTREMELY HARD TO COPY ANYONE ELSE'S WORK—INCLUDING MY OWN. WREATH MAKING, LIKE ANY OTHER ART FORM, HAS A SERENDIPITOUS QUALITY I'VE LEARNED TO ENJOY. MORE TIMES THAN NOT, THE UNPLANNED AND ACCIDENTAL THINGS THAT OCCUR RESULT IN THE MOST FUN AND BEST WORK. IT GIVES A QUALITY OF MIRTH TO YOUR DESIGN WHICH SETS IT APART FROM THE AVERAGE."

—FRED TYSON GAYLOR

THIS STUNNING
WREATH WOULD LIGHT
UP A DINING ROOM
TABLE BEAUTIFULLY,
BUT WE LIKED THE WAY
IT ADDED INTIMACY TO
THE LIVING ROOM.

MAKE BOUQUETS of dried
flowers, using primarily
hydrangea, wild roses,
and other flowers, and
glue them to a straw
base covered with
Spanish moss. Add the
artificial fruit (grapes,
pears, and plums),
using floral pins and
hot glue to secure.
Make sure to cover the
entire wreath with
flowers and fruit. Place
a candelabra or fruit
bowl in the center.

THIS GORGEOUS ARTIFICIAL WREATH PERFECTLY COMPLEMENTS THE FABRIC IN THE ARM-CHAIR, AND THE LATTICE BASE ECHOES THE STENCILED WOODWORK IN THE GLASS DOOR.

START BY wiring ivy to the inner edge of the vine base. The base is a main design element of the wreath so be sure not to hide the scalloped edges. Glue on bits of moss to cover the wire. Wire on the large tulips and the large and small mums. Next, wire on the berry clusters. Glue or wire on the miniature roses and greenery in clusters. Finish the wreath with a very light dusting of ferns and baby's breath.

"WHEN YOU'RE CHOOSING COLORS FOR A WREATH, THE GOAL IS NOT TO MAKE A PERFECT MATCH. RATHER YOU'RE LOOKING FOR HARMONIZING HUES THAT REALLY WORK TOGETHER."
—CYNTHIA GILLOOLY

THIS FRESH FLOWER
WREATH BRINGS
DRAMATIC COLOR AND
LINE TO AN APPEALING
WINDOW NOOK,
AND WOULD MAKE
AN ELEGANT CENTER-
PIECE ON A DINING
ROOM TABLE.

WIRE TWO floral cages
to a 22-inch (56 cm.)
grapevine wreath.
Fashion two identical
arrangements with
these fresh flowers and
foliage: cockscomb,
rattail celosia, golden
aster, Liatris, zinnia,
statice, galax, leather-
leaf fern and turkey
brush. Insert the tall
birch twigs. Glue on
Spanish moss to create
nests; on each side, glue
on a bird made from
mushrooms (the other
bird is looking out
the window).

Bursts of pink flowers nestled amidst lush, varied greenery contribute to the distinctive freshness of this silk wreath.

WIRE A foam cage (round floral foam covered with plastic) to the bottom right-hand corner of a 22-inch (56 cm.) grapevine wreath. Wire on the philodendron plants. Place a lotus flower, fuchsia flowers, and a large pod into the floral cage. Place a silver-king artemisia plant above the lotus flower. Diagonally above this focal point, fashion a bouquet with fuchsia, berries, and some Virginia creeper, and wire this cluster onto the wreath. Wire the pink dogwood to either side of the large flower groupings. Glue on touches of moss to cover any exposed wreath base. This wreath also works if you hang it with the lotus flower in the upper left-hand corner. Either way, the key to the wreath is the off-center positioning of the two large flower clusters.

THIS DRIED FLOWER WREATH ILLUSTRATES HOW ELEGANT A SIMPLE DESIGN CAN BE, THANKS IN PART TO THE NAVY BOW—A CLASSIC LOOK THAT'S ALWAYS IN FASHION.

COVER A wire frame with small bunches of scrap artemisia held in place with monofilament. Glue on dried lemon leaves all around the wreath. Then, starting at the top of the wreath, glue on clusters of artemisia down the sides to meet at the bottom. Glue on blue salvia in a crescent shape, covering about three-quarters of the wreath, adding delphinium blossoms near the base. To finish, wire on a navy bow.

"RIBBON IN A WREATH SHOULD BE AN INTEGRAL PART OF THE DESIGN RATHER THAN AN ADORNMENT PLACED ON TOP. THE RIBBON SHOULD APPEAR TO HAVE A FUNCTIONAL VALUE AS WELL AS BEING DECORATIVE. ITS PLACEMENT IN THE FOCAL POINT IS CRUCIAL BECAUSE THAT IS WHERE ALL THE LINES OF THE WREATH SEEM TO CONVERGE."

—FRED TYSON GAYLOR

"I PREFER SILK FLOWERS TO DRIED BECAUSE THEY ARE SO VERSATILE: I CAN COLOR THEM ANY COLOR I WANT. I CAN SPRAY THE FLOWERS AND THE BASE WITH METALLIC GOLD PAINT TO GIVE THE WREATH AN ANTIQUE LOOK. SILKS CAN BE VERY LIFELIKE, AND THEY DON'T FALL APART WHEN YOU HANDLE THEM. IF IT'S DONE RIGHT, SILK FLOWERS CAN LOOK LIKE REAL FLOWERS. THE TRICK IS TO BEND, TWIST AND ANGLE THEM SO THEY COPY THE WAY REAL FLOWERS GROW."

—NICOLE VICTORIA

PEACH POINSETTIAS AND GLIMMERS OF GOLD IN THIS SILK WREATH CHEERFULLY HERALD THE CHRISTMAS SEASON.

START WITH a 24-inch (61 cm.) wired poly-silk evergreen base. First, glue the silk poinsettias into the greenery. Weave the peach ribbon into the wreath and behind the poinsettias, then do the same with the gold lace ribbon, using picks or glue to secure the ribbons. Glue on the berries, gold ribbon, and white sparkle caspia. Add the variegated round ivy. To enhance the wreath's elegance, add glass balls and gold tassels.

DINING ROOM

A DOUBLE HELPING OF DELICATE PARCHMENT ROSES SERVED ON DOUBLE VINE RINGS MAKE THIS WREATH A PERFECT ACCOMPANIMENT TO ANY MEAL.

WIRE AN 8-inch (20 cm.) grapevine wreath base to an 18-inch (46 cm.) grapevine base. Glue German statice around the outside of the large wreath and along the bottom of the inside wreath. Glue on the miniature parchment roses and Queen Anne's lace, mirroring the pattern of the statice. You may want to finish the wreath with a floral cotton bow and hang the wreath with the rings positioned one on top of the other.

A HALO OF BAY, AUSTRALIAN CORK, AND EUCALYPTUS LEAVES SPRAYED GOLD, COPPER, AND BRONZE CREATES AN ELEGANT WREATH THAT WOULD MAKE ANYONE FEEL LIKE DRESSING FOR DINNER. THE BLACK BRAID PROVIDES CONTRAST AND COMPLETES THE CIRCLE FORM.

SPRAY THE LEAVES first (outdoors, please) with floral spray paint, but keep some of the leaves natural. Make a template 14 inches (36 cm.) in diameter on heavy paper, and trace it onto a foam core board. Cut out the form and spray it with one of the gold sprays so that you completely cover the white foam board. Next, glue on the black braid. To camouflage the sides of the base, glue on Spanish moss. Then, glue on the leaves in a downward direction towards the bottom. Lastly, glue on a favorite flower blossom sprayed black and the eucalyptus seed pods.

THERE'S A DRAMATIC, ANGULAR AIR TO THIS FRESH FLOWER WREATH THAT MAKES IT SEEM RIGHT AT HOME IN A CONTEMPORARY AND SPARE SETTING.

WIRE A twig wreath on top of a root wreath base. Insert fresh calla lilies and white Liatris into water tubes, and position the tubes into the base. Glue on purple statice and galax leaves. Tie on a raffia bow. Lastly, glue Spanish moss around the stems of the flowers.

AN ORIENTAL
WREATH THIS BEAUTI-
FUL AND UNUSUAL IS
CERTAINLY SUITABLE
FOR FRAMING.

GLUE A PIECE of floral foam onto the bottom of a picture frame and wrap it with a piece of wire for extra stability. To achieve the oriental design, insert the silk flowers into the foam in the following order: rust flowers; sunflower, sponge, mushroom and berries (the focal point); eucalyptus; white flowers and marigolds. Cut stems off turkey brush (green dried foliage) in several pieces, and position the long ones to go behind the rust flowers, the medium ones to go behind the marigolds, and the short pieces to place around the focal point.

"THERE IS NO REASON WREATHS HAVE TO BE CONSTRUCTED ON CONVENTIONAL STRAW OR STYROFOAM FORMS, OR FOR THAT MATTER EVEN GRAPEVINE. I ENJOY CUTTING OUT FORMS FROM PLYWOOD TO CREATE OVALS, LATTICES, AND OTHER SHAPES."

—FRED TYSON GAYLOR

THE PALETTE OF PINKS AND PURPLES IN THIS GRACEFUL DRIED WREATH PLAYS OFF BEAUTIFULLY AGAINST THE SILVERY BACKGROUND.

COVER A wire frame with bunches of artemisia wound tightly around the base with monofilament. Beginning at the top of the wreath, arrange clusters of dried herbs and flowers so that the fullest clusters are at the base. Glue on the artemisia and larkspur buds, and then add the other herbs and flowers: roses, carnations, feverfew, delphinium, strawflowers, grasses, and pepperberries. Wire on a full ribbon at the bottom, and pin on a loop of ribbon at the top.

THIS MAGNIFICENT, OVAL TABLE WREATH IS GRAND IN BOTH SCALE AND DESIGN, BLENDING MANY CONTRASTING MATERIALS INTO A VISUALLY APPEALING WHOLE.

GLUE SHEET MOSS onto a 24-inch (61 cm.) oval grapevine wreath. Insert twigs covered with dried fungi (that you've found on a walk through the woods). Glue on or pick in the flowers and fruits: silk alstroemeria, silk buttercups, dried sarracenia lilies, latex poppies, latex berries, figs, and grapes, and dried pepperberries. Artfully weave a wired gold mesh ribbon through this distinctive table garden.

"FLORAL DESIGN IS LIKE BAKING: SOME DAYS YOUR BISCUITS RISE PERFECTLY. OTHER DAYS THEY JUST DON'T HAVE THE JAZZ. INSPIRATION AND CREATIVITY ARE DEFINITELY AN EBB AND FLOW LIKE THE TIDES."
—CYNTHIA GILLOOLY

THIS WREATH IS A MAGNIFICENT MARRIAGE OF SUBTLE COLOR AND DYNAMIC FORM. THE WREATH SEEMS TO BE IN MOTION, THANKS TO THE DESIGNER'S USE OF SPIRAL PATTERNS, DIVERSE TEXTURES, AND THE PLACEMENT OF DRIED FLOWERS AT DIFFERENT HEIGHTS.

THE WREATH is made with a 14-inch (36 cm.) grapevine base. Use hot glue and wire to attach the dried flowers. Start with the olive branches, making sure the leaves hang gracefully. Attach clusters of larkspur next at varying heights. Attach the sweet Annie and salal leaves. Next come the orientalis, dusty miller and sarracenia lilies. Create the focal point of the wreath with dark magnolia leaves and glue them on, then wire on the cobra lilies to encircle them. Glue the delicate dogwood blossoms onto birch twigs and glue them in last.

THIS FRESH WREATH, THOUGH ITS BEAUTY IS FLEETING, STEALS THE SHOW WHEN DISPLAYED WITH THIS PRIZED COLLECTION OF ORIGINAL ART.

UNDERNEATH this summer garden is a 20-inch (51 cm.) wire base wrapped with floral tape. Wire together bunches of flowers, including yellow patrinia, white aster, flowering cinammon basil, zinnia, perennial ageratum, heliotrope, house leek, and garlic chives. Wire these bunches onto the base. To fill in any gaps, glue on several dahlia and zinnia heads.

FAMILY
ROOM

"THE UNDERLYING STRUCTURE OF A WREATH IS AS IMPORTANT TO ITS DESIGN AS IN ANY OTHER TYPE OF CONSTRUCTION. THE GLUE GUN HAS REVOLUTION-IZED WREATH MAKING, BUT IT CAN NEVER BE A SUB-STITUTE FOR THE SOUND MECHANICS NEEDED FOR OVERALL STABILITY."
—FRED TYSON GAYLOR

CAPTURE THE OLD-WORLD BEAUTY OF FLEMISH ART WITH THIS STUNNING AND DISTINCTIVE FLOWER AND FRUIT WREATH.

———◼———

USE A JIGSAW to cut out an oval from 1/2-inch (1.3 cm.) plywood, and paint it with grey or green acrylic primer. Glue silk leaves on inner and outer edges of the base and then cover the center with leaves. Affix larger pieces of vinyl fruit; (slice the bottom off the fruit to have a flat surface to glue to plywood). Glue on silk flowers, nuts, pine cones, and smaller pieces of fruit.

BRUSH ON two coats of a procelain setting agent. When dry, spray the entire wreath with a light coat of glossy, wood-tone spray paint. Dry-brush gold acrylic paint on the elevated portions of the fruit, flowers, pine cones, and leaves. Lastly, spray the wreath with matte sealer.

RECREATE THE FRAGILE SPLENDOR OF A SUMMER'S MORNING WITH THIS EXQUISITE DRIED FLOWER WREATH

———◼———

START WITH a crimped wire frame, and cover it with Spanish moss held on by monofilament. Wire lemon leaves onto the base with the leaves angled in the same direction. Fashion three bouquets comprised of dried roses, hydrangea, globe amaranth, carnations, strawflowers, cockscomb, nigella, and grasses. Glue these arrangements onto the leaves, spacing them so the entire wreath is well blanketed.

DELLA ROBBIA
FRUITS AND A PEACH
BOW IMPART A TIMELESS
CHARM TO THIS
COLORFUL WREATH.

HOT-GLUE glycerin-
preserved beech leaves
in a crescent shape onto
a grapevine wreath.
Tuck in blueberry twigs,
then add wired Della
Robbia fruit halves.
Glue on dried astilbe
spikes and strawflowers.
Lastly, wire on three
yards (2.74 m.) of heavy
cotton ribbon.

Strong lines and bold colors combine to create a wreath that is large in both scale and in impression. It also has a masculine look, which makes it a perfect wreath for a man's study or office.

◼

You'll need a grapevine wreath that's at least 26 inches (66 cm.) in diameter to provide the pheasant with an adequate nesting spot. Cut sprays of eucalyptus to lengths between 12 to 16 inches (30.5 cm. - 41 cm.), wire them into clusters and wire them to the base. Hot-glue the gold, stiffened ribbon "leaves" into place. Wrap Bunny's tail with floral tape and glue to the base. Glue on a few real pheasant feathers. Secure the pheasant to the bottom of the wreath with glue, and create its nest by gluing on Spanish moss. Wire on a bountiful bow at the top, letting the ribbon drape down the sides.

Do you enjoy curling up under a tree with a good book? This lovely wreath doesn't offer any shade, but it does create an inviting place for reading day or night.

MAKE A LARGE and a small raffia bow and attach them with wire to a 14-inch (36 cm.) fern root wreath. Leave long streamers on the smaller bow and let them trail down so it looks like the two bows are connected. Glue or wire on the pomegranates. Glue on ivy, using a long piece to cross over the wreath center to join with the opposite cluster. Lastly, glue on small, rust-colored blossoms.

"MAKE SURE THAT THE WREATH YOU MAKE COMPLEMENTS THE AREA IN WHICH IT WILL HANG. MATCH THE STYLE OF WREATH TO THE TYPE OF DECOR. THE DECOR WILL HELP DETERMINE COLORS AND TEXTURE TO BE USED IN THE WREATH."

—JULIANNE BRONDER

THIS WHITE ON WHITE DRIED FLOWER WREATH WITH JUST A HINT OF COLOR COMES ALIVE AGAINST THE WALLPAPER IN THIS FRIENDLY, SUNNY ROOM.

CUT A BLOCK of floral foam into two thin, rectangular pieces and press them into a 14-inch (36 cm.) three-ring wire base. Trim away the excess and continue pressing the foam pieces into the base until it is completely filled. Cover the base with Spanish moss and secure it with thin-gauge floral wire.

FIRST INSERT the German statice around the outside of the entire wreath. Make bundles of all the flowers on floral picks: white roses, wild baby's breath, silver-king artemisia, white yarrow, feverfew, boneset, oats, ammobium, lamb's ears, and fountain grass. Work clockwise and from the outside to the inside and then the middle. Add the strawflowers and blue salvia to provide contrast. Lastly, glue an organdy ribbon to a pick and insert it into the base.

"WHEN YOU'RE CHOOSING COLORS FOR A WREATH, THE GOAL IS NOT TO MAKE A PERFECT MATCH. RATHER YOU'RE LOOKING FOR HARMONIZING HUES THAT REALLY WORK TOGETHER."

—CYNTHIA GILLOOLY

T<small>HIS WREATH IS</small>
<small>NOT FOR THE FAINT-</small>
<small>HEARTED. I</small>T'<small>S LIKE THE</small>
<small>WINDSWEPT PRAIRIES: IMPRES-</small>
<small>SIVELY LARGE, BEAUTIFUL,</small>
<small>AND WILD. (H</small><small>INT: YOU CAN</small>
<small>USE THE SAME INGREDIENTS</small>
<small>AND MAKE THE WREATH ON A</small>
<small>SMALLER SCALE.)</small>

P<small>URCHASE</small> 16 feet (5 m.) of aluminum gutter guard, and roll it into a tube. Then fashion it into an oval by wiring the two ends together. Cover the base with Spanish moss secured to the aluminum with heavy-gauge wire. Go out on a field trip to the nearest meadow or perhaps your own backyard and gather whatever wild grasses strike your fancy. Create bunches with these grasses, and wire them onto the base in a spiral direction. Overlap the bunches to completely cover any wire or the base itself. Then fashion the two focal points at the top and bottom by gluing on white larkspur, bracken fern, wild grasses, hydrangea, and bear grass. Make sure the materials angle out from the wreath like star bursts. Then fill in the rest of the wreath with these materials in a spiral direction.

KITCHEN

A DELICATE PALETTE OF PASTEL COLORS DECORATES THIS SIMPLE AND ELEGANT PAPER RIBBON WREATH.

CURL FOUR YARDS (3.66 m.) of twisted paper ribbon in the desired loop shape and secure with covered wire. On a flat surface, fashion a spray from the lilacs, roses, and heather, and wire them together. Then wire the spray to the upper tier of paper ribbon loops. Secure a second, smaller cluster of flowers, and wire it to form the lower bouquet.

SECURE A BUNCH of fresh grapes by inserting the stem into a grapevine base. Glue on lettuce leaves and ferns. Insert sunflowers and caspia into water tubes that are positioned in the base.

"I LIKE WORKING WITH
FRESH FLOWERS BECAUSE
I LIKE DESIGNS THAT
CAPTURE THE NATURAL
LOOK OF A GARDEN.
IT'S IMPORTANT TO KEEP
THE FLOWERS FRESH-
LOOKING AS LONG AS
POSSIBLE. BE SURE TO BUY
THEM AT A FLORIST SHOP
WHERE THEY'VE BEEN
SPECIALLY TREATED TO
LAST LONGER. OR, IF
YOU'RE USING FLOWERS
FROM YOUR GARDEN, YOU
CAN EXTEND THEIR LIFE BY
ADDING A TABLESPOON OF
BLEACH TO A GALLON OF
WATER AND PUTTING THE
FLOWERS IN THAT LIQUID
UNTIL YOU'RE READY TO
USE THEM IN A WREATH.
THE BLEACH KEEPS THE
BACTERIA DOWN AND
SLOWS THE DETERIORA-
TION PROCESS."

—TOMMY WALLEN

A MEDLEY OF DRIED HERBS CREATES AN EYE-CATCHING COMBINATION OF COLOR, SHAPE, AND TEXTURE IN THIS KITCHEN WREATH.

COVER A WIRE frame with artemisia by taking small bunches of the herb and binding it tightly to the wire with monofilament. Glue on silver-king and silver-queen artemisia, and then add the following herbs: sage, safflower, basil flowers, feverfew, bay leaves, oregano, tansy, chives, and lamb's ears.

"DRY HEAT AND AIR CONDITIONING TAKE MOISTURE OUT OF DRIED FLOWERS AND CAN MAKE THEM EXTREMELY BRITTLE AND FRAGILE. SOME FLOWERS SUCH AS STATICE CAN BE REVIVED BY SPRAYING WATER ON THEM WITH A SPRAY ATOMIZER AND PLACING THEM IN A PLASTIC BAG FOR HALF AN HOUR UNTIL THEY ABSORB ENOUGH MOISTURE TO ALLOW YOU TO WORK WITH THEM. EXPERIMENT WITH OTHER FLOWERS; SOME HERBS SUCH AS OREGANO AND MINT WILL TURN BLACK WITH THIS METHOD."

—BARBARA APPLEBAUM

THE SYMMETRICAL
PLACEMENT OF
MATERIALS AND THE
HARMONIZING HUES OF
CRANBERRY CREATE A
DELIGHTFULLY PLEASING
KITCHEN ADORNMENT.

COVER A straw wreath
with Spanish moss,
using monofilament to
secure the moss. Glue
on a generous forest
of glycerin-preserved
beech leaves. Then
arrange and glue on the
Della Robbia grapes,
pomegranates, berries,
and other fruits. Lastly,
glue on the dried astilbe
and oregano blossoms.

FEW FLOWERS EVOKE
THE PLEASURE OF SUMMER
DAYS AS READILY AS BLACK-
EYED SUSANS AND SUN-
FLOWERS, AND THIS SILK
WREATH IS A HANGING
GARDEN OF THEM.

WRAP GREEN floral tape
around a 12-inch (30.5
cm.) straw wreath base.
Assemble bunches of silk
laurel leaves, and secure
them onto 3-inch long
(7.6 cm.) floral picks. To
establish the outline of the
wreath, insert the laurel
bunches into the base,
positioning half to angle
in one direction and the
other half in the opposite
direction. Both lines of
leaves should meet at a
point opposite from where
you'll position the bow,
which is the wreath's focal
point. Cover the top and
inside of the wreath form
with laurel clusters, keep-
ing the same two direc-
tions. Secure the stems of
the sunflowers to picks
and insert them into the
wreath. Attach the black-
eyed Susans and yellow
cosmos in the same man-
ner. Make a bow from
maize yellow cotton rib-
bon and attach it to the
base with floral wire.

THIS APPETIZING
WREATH ACHIEVES ITS
DYNAMIC EFFECT FROM
THE DIVERSE COLORS,
TEXTURES, AND
PROPORTIONS OF THE
INGREDIENTS.

WIRE TWO STRAINERS at
an angle to a 22-inch
(56 cm.) oval grapevine
wreath. Position the silk
celery and latex kale so
that the kale overlaps
the large strainer. Tie a
raffia bow and attach it
to the celery with glue
or wire. Attach the
celery and kale to the
wreath with wire, and
glue on the violet bush
below these vegetables.
Glue on the ivy around
the small strainer.
Attach the pods and the
cosmos with wire or
glue. Secure the roses
above the kale, making
sure to follow the line
of the strainer handles.
Lastly, glue bits of moss
to the outer edge of the
wreath. Note: Avoid
hanging this wreath in
direct sunshine as it will
cause the latex kale to
break down.

WRAP A WIRE wreath with floral tape. Assemble several bundles of broomcorn in a variety of colors and use wire or floral tape to hold them together. Determine where you want the basket to hang and leave that space available. Attach the bundles of broomcorn to the base with floral wire. Next, wire on the basket, making sure to balance the wreath so that it doesn't pull down on the side with the basket. Wire into the basket the following: bundles of wheat, rye, and oats; white and purple oregano; sweet marjoram, and mountain mint. Add to the basket chives, star anise, and purple bee balm, glued in one at a time. Glue in the 12-inch (30.5 cm.) cinnamon sticks. Attach the garlic to the outside of the basket with glue and wire. Glue on the cayenne and chili peppers. Glue the cereal grains around the wreath in between the broomcorn. Use the raffia to tie together bundles of 6-inch (15 cm.) cinnamon sticks and tie them on to the wreath. Lastly, tie the wooden utensils together with raffia and tie them onto the wreath.

THIS WREATH ILLUS-
TRATES HOW TWO VERY
DIFFERENT HALVES CAN
COMBINE TO FORM ONE
VERY DYNAMIC WHOLE.
THE BABY'S BREATH
PROVIDES AN UNDER-
STATED COMPLEMENT
TO THE THREE-
DIMENSIONAL ENERGY
OF THE DRIED FRUITS
AND FLOWERS.

GLUE SPANISH MOSS onto
a straw wreath. Cover
half with baby's breath.
Cover the other half
with dried oranges,
pomegranates, chili
peppers, garlic bulbs,
and dried flowers,
including lavender,
hydrangea, yarrow,
and seed pods.

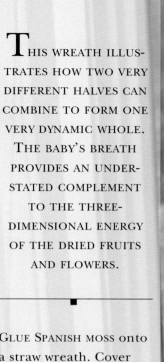

"MAGNIFICENT" SAYS IT ALL! WORKING ON A LARGE SCALE, THIS STUNNING DRIED FLOWER WREATH BURSTS WITH COLOR AND MOVEMENT. IT SUCCEEDS IN BEING BOTH EXOTIC AND ROMANTIC... DESIRABLE QUALITIES FOR A BEDROOM, DON'T YOU THINK?

THE BASE IS a 22-inch (56 cm.) grapevine wreath. Pick in the juniper berries first, spreading them out to create color flares encircling the wreath. Glue on the millet and amaranth in clusters of varying heights, with some angled out from the base and others pointing toward its center. Glue on sweet Annie next (for sweet dreams, of course), followed by the nigella pods, which so perfectly pull together the colors of the millet and amaranth. Glue on the remaining materials in this order: sprays of rye, clusters of dog-tooth violet pods, freeze-dried roses and rose leaves, water-colored caspia (maroone), and lemon leaves. To create the playful, dancing effect of the horsetail grass, bend the grass into a loop and glue it to the wreath so that the "tail" (the pointy end) is bent out from the base.

THE LADY OF THE HOUSE
(MRS. GEORGE VANDERBILT,
OWNER OF BILTMORE HOUSE)
WAS PARTIAL TO GOLD AND
PURPLE, AND WOULD NO DOUBT
HAVE ADORED THIS EXQUISITE
WREATH THAT THE DESIGNER
MADE ESPECIALLY FOR HER
ROOM. IF YOU'RE PARTIAL
TO PURPLE (AND DREAM ABOUT
GOLD), TRY CREATING THIS
GORGEOUS DRIED WREATH
FOR YOUR BEDROOM.

Wire Ti tree to a wire base. Glue on small puffs of hydrangea all around the wreath, then add bands of this flower as accents. Glue on loop bows of purple and lavender wired French ribbon. Glue on stems of blue larkspur radiating out from the bows. Be sure to stagger the stem lengths and work the shorter pieces into the hydrangea to add height and depth to the wreath. Create a garland ribbon of loop bows by catching two or three loops of the narrow metallic gold ribbon in a steel pick, skip six to eight inches (15 - 20 cm.) and catch two or three more loops. Vary the size of the loops and the bows to enhance visual interest. Put a dab of glue on the pick and push the ribbon into the hydrangea and tie to the base to accent the hydrangea circle.

Here's a stunning example of how successful a design can be that positions delicate flowers and a luminous ribbon on a large and sturdy grapevine wreath.

Start with a 24-inch (61 cm.) grapevine wreath. Glue blue silk caspia onto the wreath. Then glue on silk morning glories, small latex tulips, silk grasses, and blue silk flowers, with a full bouquet arrangement as the focal point at the bottom. Don't put any flowers on the top third of the wreath. Glue on the flocked latex ivy. Fashion a full bow with long streamers from moiré ribbon, and wire it to the top of the wreath. Drape the streamers down through this cool, blue and white forest.

"MANY TIMES IN DESIGN I START WITH ONE SPECIFIC
COMPONENT — PERHAPS A GORGEOUS RIBBON OR
MY MOST IMPORTANT FLOWER — AND THEN I BUILD
FROM THAT. OFTEN, MY COMPONENTS DON'T SEEM TO
HAVE HARMONY. I WALK AWAY FROM THE DESIGN, FOR
HOURS OR EVEN DAYS. THEN I STUDY IT VISUALLY.
ALMOST INVARIABLY, IT BECOMES APPARENT WHAT
NEEDS TO BE ADDED OR SUBTRACTED."

—CYNTHIA GILLOOLY

WOULDN'T IT BE NICE TO HAVE WILD ROSES GROWING IN YOUR BEDROOM? THIS LOVELY WREATH (ALL SILK...NO PRUNING NECESSARY) CAN MAKE THAT WISH COME TRUE.

————————————■————

LOOSELY COVER a grapevine wreath base with greenery, using glue to attach the foliage. Make sure to angle the leaves in the same direction. Attach each of the silk flowers except the tulips to floral picks and glue them to the base in the following order: wild roses in different colors, cosmos, mini-tulips (glue these on in clusters), heather, and baby's breath. The beauty of this wreath lies in its airy quality. To achieve this effect, don't cover the wreath with a solid mass of flowers and foliage, and position some of the flowers to come up out of the greenery.

THE LUSTROUS COLORS AND HARMONIOUS DESIGN OF THIS DRIED FLOWER WREATH ARE SURE TO INSPIRE SWEET DREAMS.

COVER A WIRE WREATH with scraps of artemisia, bound securely to the base with monofilament. Take small bunches of baby's breath and wire them on. Glue on the dried flowers: zinnias, hydrangea, delphinium, strawflowers, carnations, globe amaranth, blue salvia, cockscomb, and larkspur.

"YOU DON'T HAVE TO BE A TRAINED DESIGNER TO MAKE BEAUTIFUL WREATHS. CHOOSE FLOWERS AND MATERIALS YOU LIKE AND PUT PLEASING COLORS TOGETHER. THE DESIGN WILL COME AS YOU START WORKING WITH YOUR MATERIALS."

—LUCK MCELREATH

THIS WREATH IS A
WONDERFUL REMINDER
THAT THERE'S NO PLACE
LIKE HOME, ESPECIALLY
ONE WITH SUCH A
CAPTIVATING "TOTO,"
(A.K.A SU-SU) WAITING
TO JUMP IN YOUR LAP.

CUT OUT a lattice circle
from plywood with a
jigsaw and then cut out
the center. Paint or
stain the base. Fasten
the grapevine to the
perimeter of the lattice
with staples or wire.
Then, staple or wire on
the artificial black-eyed
Susans and greenery on
top of the vines.
Morning glories or
trumpet vines would
look terrific, too.
Finally, in tribute to the
Scarecrow, add a gener-
ous raffia bow.

THE HEROINE OF THIS
EXQUISITE WREATH IS
THE FRENCH RIBBON
THAT VISUALLY TIES
TOGETHER THE COLORS
OF THE SILK FLOWERS
AND DRIED FOLIAGE,
AND ENTICES YOUR EYE
TO TRAVEL ALL AROUND
THE WREATH.

Glue sheet moss onto a
grapevine wreath base.
Glue on the silk butter-
cups and Peruvian lily.
Glue on the preserved
eucalyptus, silk foliage,
and dried caspia.
Fill in with reindeer
moss. Gently weave the
French ribbon through
the wreath.

THE THREE LITTLE BEARS IN THIS WREATH, CHEERFULLY NESTLED IN AMONG THE YUMMY LOOKING BERRIES, WILL BRING A SMILE TO ANY CHILD'S FACE.

THIS IS REALLY two wreaths in one. Start with a straw wreath base (remove the plastic wrap if necessary). Take a grapevine wreath and unwind the grapevine. Lay sections of grape-vine over the straw base, securing it to the straw form by wrapping wire around it. Establish the outline by picking in silk laurel leaves, inside and out. Attach the bears to the grapevine with thin-gauge wire wrapped around the arm and leg joints of the bears. Pick in the fruit. Then add more leaves, along with lichen, moss, and silk mushrooms. The final, sweet touch is a raffia bow.

THE ADORABLE TEDDY
BEARS IN THIS WREATH
WILL KEEP A BABY
COMPANY FOR MANY
MONTHS TO COME.

WRAP A 27-inch (69 cm.)
straw wreath form (with
plastic wrap left on)
with about 10 yards
(19.14 m.) of aqua satin
ribbon. Cover the entire
form with about 25
yards (22.86 m.) of
white net, wrapping the
net in a spiral direction.
Gather the excess net at
the bottom and allow
the remainder to trail
down. To affix the plush
bears, wrap white
chenille-covered wire
around their waists.
Then wrap the ends of
the wire around metal
picks and insert them
into the wreath base.
Glue on the letters. Pick
in the silk flowers and
dried baby's breath.
Glue on the baby rattles.
Attach loops of ribbon
to metal picks and insert
them into the base.

THIS SIMPLE AND DELICATE WREATH ARTFULLY COMBINES BLUE AND PINK, MAKING IT PERFECT FOR A BABY BOY OR A BABY GIRL.

WITH PINKING SHEARS, cut blue satin material in 2-inch ((5.1 cm.) strips, and wrap them around a Styrofoam wreath, using dress-maker pins to secure. Wrap lace ribbon over the satin. Fashion a lace bow with long streamers, and wire the bow onto the wreath. Pin the streamers to the lower part of the wreath. From the pink cord, make a bow with long streamers and pin it onto the lace bow. Pin the ends of the streamers to the wreath. Glue on silk foliage and pink lilac flowers. For a final lacy touch, glue on the fern.

"IT'S IMPORTANT THAT THE WREATH BE BALANCED; WHATEVER YOU DO ON ONE SIDE NEEDS TO BE BAL-ANCED ON THE OTHER. IF, FOR EXAMPLE, YOU HAVE A LONG STEM POINTING WAY UP IN THE AIR, YOU'LL NEED TO HAVE A STEM ON THE LOWER SIDE OF THE WREATH DROPPING DOWN AWAY FROM THE WREATH."

—MICHELLE KOEPKE WEST

WITH ITS MILK-
WASHED TWIG BASE,
ORGANDY BOW, AND
SPRINKLING OF PANSIES,
THIS DRIED FLOWER
WREATH IS AS DELICATE
AND FRESH AS SPRING.

SPRAY THE WREATH with white wash floral spray. Create the background of the wreath by making clusters of dried flowers using lady's-mantle, sweet Annie, mugwort, white yarrow, and yellow moonshine yarrow. Glue the clusters to the base, leaving space at the top for the bow. Glue on bundles of white pearly everlasting, ammobium, and feverfew. Divide the wreath into thirds with pink cockscomb. Then add pink globe ama-ranth, dispersing it around the wreath so that pink is the predom-inant color. As a final blessing, glue on the fragile pansies and organdy bow.

SWEET AND RADIANT
DESCRIBE THIS NURSERY
WREATH, PERFECT
WORDS TO DESCRIBE
THE NEW BABY, TOO.

START WITH A painted
and milk-washed grape-
vine wreath. Make a bow
with long streamers from
cotton tapestry ribbon,
drape the streamers
around the wreath, and
use glue to secure them
to the base. Next, glue
dried caspia around the
bow. Tie on the shoes.
Give the baby a kiss.

THIS INGENIOUS AND
WHIMSICAL WREATH
PROVIDES A HAPPY SOLU-
TION FOR THE PARENT
WHOSE CHILD ASKS:
"CAN WE GET SOME
FISH, MOM, HUH, MOM?"

■

YOU'LL NEED A large
27-inch (69 cm.) straw
wreath covered with
plastic. Spray the entire
wreath, first with fleck-
stone spray paint, and
when dry, with purple
flat paint (or any other
color). Anchor the plas-
tic, green seaweed using
steel picks. Then, with
floral picks, insert the
silk, peach-colored
buttercups, the peach
glittered rucus (dried
and colored greenery),
and the silk, lavender
fuji mums. Gather the
green fish net, picking
it in behind the mums.
Complete your under-
water scene by gluing
on tropical fish and
sea shells.

VISUAL INTEREST IS ACHIEVED IN THIS BEAUTIFUL WREATH BY COMBINING FRESH FLOWERS AND FOLIAGE THAT SHOW OFF NATURE'S WILDLY DIVERSE RANGE OF COLORS AND TEXTURES.

TO MAKE THE BASE, cover an 8-inch (20 cm.) plastic ring with florist tape. Wire on 2-inch (5 cm.) bunches of German statice. Overlap each bunch just enough to cover the stems of the preceeding bunch. Hot glue other decorative material onto the statice base. Begin with the larger, more prominent flowers, and work down to the smaller items. Try to glue flowers and foliage deep inside and outside the wreath to create a three-dimensional look. The fresh flowers and foliage include pink cockscomb, pink strawflowers, white annual statice, hydrangea, marjoram, and jade (long green leaves are available from wholesale florists).

"WHEN WORKING WITH DRIED FLOWERS, NEVER WORRY WHETHER A STEM IS TOO SHORT. YOU CAN ALWAYS LENGTHEN IT BY USING A WIRE AND FLORAL TAPE, A PICK, OR BY TAPING THE FLOWER TO THE STEM OF A STRONGER FLOWER. FLORAL TAPE IS VERY NECESSARY WITH DRIED FLOWERS. LEARN HOW TO USE IT. IT STRENGTHENS AS YOU PULL IT DOWN AROUND STEMS, WIRE, ETC."

—BARBARA APPLEBAUM

THIS SWEET-LOOKING
AND SWEET-SMELLING
WREATH WILL CERTAINLY
CHARM SOME LUCKY
GIRL TO DREAMLAND.

FIRST ATTACH the irre-
sistible cherub to a eucalyptus wreath by tying
ribbon around its neck
in a bow and then tying
to the back of the
wreath. Glue on the
dried berries next.
You'll need three yards
(1.83 m.) each of all
three colors of ribbon.
Cut two yards (2.74 m.)
each of light pink and
medium pink satin rib-
bon, and weave the
strands around the
wreath and under the
leaves. Cut three pieces
of dark pink silk ribbon,
1/2 yard long (46 cm.),
and fashion each piece
into a full bow. Glue
bows on at the sides and
at the top. Use the
remaining ribbon in all
three shades to make a
bow for the bottom of
the wreath and glue
in place.

THIS LOVELY WREATH, DISPLAYED IN THE SHERIDAN ROOM IN BILTMORE HOUSE, ACHIEVES A LATE SUMMER, EARLY FALL FEELING, THROUGH THE ARTFUL COMBINATION OF GOLD AND RUST-COLORED DRIED AND SILK MATERIALS.

START WITH a twig wreath base and glue on bunches of dried golden hydrangea, Australian daisies, and sweet Annie. Accent with pieces of dried, soft wooly mullein and various grasses. Glue on silk zinnias and add waxed fall leaves. Lastly, glue on a gold metallic bow and catch the streamers to the side. (A dab of glue will hold the ribbon in place.)

GUEST ROOM

BY SELECTING DRIED MATERIALS
IN MUTED SHADES OF CREAM AND
GREEN, THE DESIGNER CREATED
A DELICATE WREATH THAT
BEAUTIFULLY COMPLEMENTS THE
LACE CURTAINS, AND WOULD MELT
THE HEART OF ANY SPECIAL GUEST.

START WITH A ready-made dried bay
leaf base. Glue on bits and pieces
of the following flowers and
foliage: white delphinium,
Australian daisy, white Ti tree,
santolina, eucalyptus leaves and
berries, small green thistles, Scotch
broom, globe thistle, bracken fern,
artemisia, caspia, and dusty miller.
Vary the heights of these materials
to give depth to the wreath. Choose
some of the heavier materials and
glue them on in bands, rather than
scattering them throughout the
wreath. Place shades of cream and
green from the lightest to the dark-
est. To create a focal point, use the
longest stemmed materials and
angle them to swoop forward
toward the table surface.

THIS WREATH PROVES THAT HAPPY MARRIAGES CAN BE BASED ON THE ATTRACTION OF OPPOSITES. THE DELICATE LACE LOOKS QUITE AT HOME ON THE ROUGH GRAPEVINE (AS DOES THE LITTLE BIRD!).

PURCHASE OR MAKE the cotton hat. Fold the hat into a basket shape, and glue the top to a grapevine base. Fill the basket with flowers, dried or artificial. Glue on the wide lace bow, and let the ribbon streamers drape down the front of the basket. Fashion a second bow from thin satin ribbon, and glue onto the first ribbon. Glue on a rose, zinnia, or your favorite flower. Add greenery and other flowers and let them flow down from the basket. Secure with hot glue. Lastly, glue on the bird and some greenery.

"I START BY SHOPPING TO SEE WHAT CATCHES MY EYE, AND THAT WILL BE THE FOCAL POINT—MAYBE A SEA SHELL OR A SANTA CLAUS OR A MAGNOLIA IN BLOOM. THEN I LOOK FOR OTHER MATERIALS THAT WILL COMPLEMENT IT, AND SET IT OFF IN AN APPEALING WAY."

—MICHELLE KOEPKE WEST

GUESTS MAY NOT
WANT TO LEAVE
WHEN THEY SEE THIS
BEAUTIFUL WREATH
BLOOMING WITH
SOUTHERN CHARM.

THE SILK MAGNOLIA
leaves are the stars of
the wreath, so wire a
generous quantity to a
14-inch (35.6 cm.) box
base. Wire on the mag-
nolia blossoms, lilies,
and wild roses. Hot-glue
Spanish moss to the
wreath form, using
small bunches until the
base is covered.

THIS INNOVATIVE WREATH ECHOES THE LOOK OF THE BRASS BED, AND THE BOUQUETS OF FLOWERS SOFTEN THE ANGLES.

CUT BAMBOO into two 3-foot (91.4 cm.) lengths and two 2-foot (61 cm.) lengths. Spray the bamboo with gold paint. Join the four corners with nails. Wire on blocks of floral foam at opposing corners, and cover the foam by gluing on Spanish moss. Insert silk magnolias and lilies, dried Liatris and statice, artificial apples sprays and blackberries, and gilded Queen Anne's lace. For a final surprise element, glue single sprays of blackberries in opposite corners.

GRANDMA'S ROOM

THIS NOVELTY WREATH CAN BE PERSONALIZED BY ADDING MEMENTOS THAT EXPRESS TO GRANDMA JUST HOW SPECIAL YOU THINK SHE IS.

THERE'S A BOX wreath base under all those little pillows. To make the pillows, cut out fabric squares measuring four -1/2 inches by five inches (11.4 cm. - 12.7 cm.), fill them with polyester stuffing and sew them together. Attach the pillows to the wire base by tying each one on with ribbon. Make three heart-shaped pillows and glue them together. Attach these to the base with ribbon. Glue on the chair, lace sachet, and miniature sewing basket. Tie on an embroidered handkerchief. Pin on the old-timey greeting card, and add other items if you desire.

"I SOMETIMES FIND INSPIRATION FOR WREATHS BY LOOKING AT MY 'SCRAP BOX' WHERE I KEEP SMALL, BROKEN AND LEFTOVER PIECES FROM PREVIOUS PROJECTS."
—**CATHY BARNHARDT**

BATHROOM

THIS GILDED FLORAL
BOUQUET ADDS OLD-
WORLD CHARM TO
A POWDER ROOM.

GLUE ON SILK greenery
to the lower center of a
vine base. Cut off the
yellow silk roses from
the stems and glue them
on. Glue on plum silk
flowers so that it looks
like they are growing up
the side of the wreath.
Loop three yards (2.74
m.) of lavender satin
ribbon and tie a bow in
the center. Glue on yel-
low silk flower blossoms.
Hang the wreath on a
wall protected by paper,
and spray the base with
metallic gold paint. Be
sure to lightly spray the
flowers to highlight
them with gold, too.

"I LIKE TO WORK WITH
CONTRASTING COLORS AND
TEXTURES BECAUSE IT ADDS
VISUAL INTEREST. SO IF I HAVE
SOME HARD PODS, I'LL USE SILK
FLOWERS, TOO, AND MAYBE INCOR-
PORATE DRIED MATERIALS, TOO."

—MICHELLE KOEPKE WEST

COMBINING DRIED FLOWERS AND SILK FOLIAGE OF DIFFERENT HEIGHTS AND TEXTURES CREATES A DISTINCTIVE AND BEAUTIFUL BATHSIDE WREATH.

COVER A GRAPEVINE wreath with sheet moss, using glue to secure. Glue on the flowers and foliage: silk variegated ivy, dried yellow roses, lemon leaves, sarracenia lilies, German statice, and pepperberries.

THIS DISTINCTIVE WREATH BEAUTIFULLY ECHOES THE ANTIQUE ELEGANCE OF THE ROOM.

SPRAY A VINE WREATH with oxide red primer, and when it's dry, with metallic antique gold. Fashion a bow from a length of gold cording and glue it to the base. Position the ivy leaves (these are teal-colored parchment brushed with gold), and secure them with hot glue. Lastly, glue on the blue grapes. The grape clusters can become either the top or the bottom of the wreath depending on how and where you choose to display it.

THE ANTIQUE LOOKING, HANDMADE DOLL IS THE SCENE STEALER IN THIS DAINTY POWDER ROOM WREATH.

TO MAKE THE DOLL, dye a linen handkerchief and some lace trim in tea. When the fabric is dry, sew on the lace trim. Use a small amount of polyester fill for the head, and keep the shape by tying thread around the neck. Make the bonnet by gluing or sewing lace around the doll's head. Loop a strand of satin ribbon around its head and make a bow at the doll's neck. Fold the hankie in half, and bring the corners up to make the arms. Glue the arms to the doll's waist, then glue on a ribbon rose to the doll's "hands." Glue flowers into a miniature basket, and loop the basket through the doll's arm. Then, attach the doll to the grapevine base with ribbon. Wrap more ribbon around the waist to create a bow. Adorn the wreath with pearls. Glue on aritifcial roses and other tiny flowers of your choice. To complete the pretty setting, glue on two satin ribbon bows.

"WHEN YOU'RE WORKING WITH DRIED FLOWERS, I FIND IT WORKS TO SPRAY THE COMPLETED WREATH WITH A MATTE SEALER TO HELP IT LAST LONGER."

—JEANNETTE HAFNER

THIS DELICATE AND
FEMININE DRIED FLOWER
WREATH IS A CHARMING
COMPLEMENT TO ANY
WOMAN WHO, LIKE
VENUS, EMERGES
REFRESHED AND ROSY
FROM HER BATH.

COVER A WIRE WREATH
with scraps of artemisia
wound tightly around
the base with monofila-
ment. Completely blan-
ket the base with bunch-
es of baby's breath. Into
this soft blanket, tuck
the following dried
flowers: carnations,
globe amaranth, roses,
strawflowers, cocks-
comb, nigella, and
silver-king artemisia.
Unfurl the ribbon
through the wreath,
fashion a full bow and
glue it on.

Imitate the look of Della Robbia sculpture with this beautiful, terra cotta wreath, an art form developed by a Florentine family in the 15th Century and exhibited in many cathedrals and museums around the world.

With a jigsaw, cut out an oval from 1/2-inch (1.3 cm.) plywood and paint it with red oxide primer. Glue on outer and inner rows of artificial leaves, and then fill in the center with additional leaves. Cut the fruit so that it has a flat side, and glue down the large pieces first. Fill in with smaller fruit and flowers, leaving room for a bow. Tie a cotton bow with streamers and glue in place. Complete the fruit and flower arrangement so that the bow is integrated into the design, rather than sitting on top. Glue a large rose onto the bow.

Coat the entire wreath with a porcelain setting agent and allow to dry. (Decoupage medium can be used.) Add a second coat. When the wreath is completely dry, apply two or more thick coats of burnt sienna acrylic gesso, filling in cracks and crevices. Mix burnt sienna acrylic paint with a small amount of white plus a dab of yellow ocher and paint entire wreath. Let wreath dry. Add a little more white and ocher and sponge on this lighter tone with a dry sponge to highlight the raised sections. Add another dab of white and yellow ocher and highlight the rose and bow. Allow wreath to dry and spray with a matte sealer.

Here's a simple wreath that demonstrates an attractive, novel way to use potpourri. Fragrance can be restored with aerosol spray.

Brush on a thick coat of glue to a molded Styrofoam wreath form. Sprinkle potpourri over the wreath, making sure to imbed the larger pieces into the glue. Glue additional dried or pressed flowers on top of this layer, then attach a bright bow.

"Always keep your dried flowers, especially those dried in silica gel, in a closed container with a desiccant until the summer humidity has passed."

—Jeannette Hafner

THIS BEAUTIFUL WREATH MIRRORS THE WAY SPRING BULBS GROW UP FROM THE GROUND. APPEALING, VERTICAL LINES AND LUMINOUS SILK FLOWERS ENHANCE THE BATHER'S VIEW.

———————————

UNWRAP A FEW STRANDS from the inside of a 12-inch (30.5 cm.) vine wreath, and wire to them a foam cage (round floral foam wrapped in a plastic cage). Put the hyacinth into an empty bulb. Glue several pieces of palm foliage into the other bulb. Glue one bulb to the side of the cage. Add the second bulb on top of the cage, first by inserting the wire at the bottom of the bulb into the foam and then using glue to reenforce. Cover the foam cage with sheet moss or Spanish moss. Insert other flowers into the foam in this order: crocus, lilacs, and baby's breath. Insert stems of peppergrass between the crocus. Fill in the space with greenery and finish the wreath with touches of moss.

"WHETHER YOU'RE WORKING WITH DRIED OR ARTIFICIAL FLOWERS, I THINK IT'S IMPORTANT TO USE FLOWERS THAT NORMALLY BLOOM AT THE SAME TIME. THIS GIVES THE WREATH A CERTAIN LOGIC AND SUBTLE, SEASONAL FEELING."

—FRED TYSON GAYLOR

MUSIC ROOM

*HOW TO ANTIQUE
SHEET MUSIC

1. Wipe brown wax shoe polish lightly over sheet music.

2. Accordion fold music sheet.

3. Lightly singe the edges of music sheet with lit match.

4. Put transparent tape over the center fold (so that wire won't cut into the paper).

THIS WREATH DEFINITELY STRIKES THE PERFECT CHORD FOR THAT SPECIAL ROOM WHERE FRIENDS AND FAMILY ENJOY MAKING MUSIC TOGETHER.

ANTIQUE TWO SHEETS OF MUSIC.* Make a bow with four streamers from four yards (3.66 m.) of natural sinamay ribbon. Tie a bow around a large sheet of music. Glue a small sheet of music into the center of the bow, and then tie the bow onto an 18-inch (45.7 cm.) open weave vine base. Wire on latex eucalyptus, apples, and pods. Wire on artificial greenery and a spray of silk dogwood around the bow. Finally, glue a dried mushroom onto the bow.

So CONVINCING IS THIS SILK WREATH, YOU MAY IMAGINE THE SCENT OF SPRING FLOWERS IS IN THE AIR. THE ALPHABET OF BLOOMS INCLUDES AJUGA, AZALEA, COLUMBINE, DANDELIONS, DIANTHUS, PANSIES, PRIMULAS, VIOLAS, AND VIOLETS.

USE A JIGSAW to cut out a 24-inch (61 cm.) circle from 1/2-inch (1.3 cm.) plywood, then cut out a circle inside the board three to four inches (7.6 cm. - 10 cm.) in diameter. Cut ten 3-inch (7.6 cm.) blocks out of 2-inch by 2-inch (5.1 cm. x 5.1 cm.) plywood, and angle one end of each block 45 degrees. Using a drill and Sheetrock screws and washers, attach the 45-degree cut end to the plywood base. Attach the terra cotta pots to the blocks with Sheetrock screws and washers. Cut out Styrofoam pieces to fit the wreath shape and cut it to fit around the terra cotta pots. Spread hot glue onto the base with a spatula and then lay on the Styrofoam. Staple flat bunches of foliage around the outer and inner circumferences of the base. Cover center of Styrofoam with picked bunches of silk laurel foliage. Fill the pots with small cut-to-fit pieces of styrofoam. Cover with sheet moss or Spanish moss secured with greening pins. Create flower clusters using floral picks, and insert stems into the styrofoam, establishing the outer dimensions first. Insert small plants into pots. Add bow at bottom. Glue on seed packs and insert the miniature gardening tools.

THE VIBRANT COLORS
IN THIS FRESH CELOSIA
WREATH EVOKE THE
IRRESISTIBLE PASSION
OF SUMMER.

START WITH AN 18-inch
(56 cm.) straw base
covered with Spanish
moss. Using floral pins,
completely cover the
front of the base with
cockscomb in a variety
of shades, and a few
clusters of pink sedum.

"I USUALLY WORK CLOCKWISE AND FROM THE OUTSIDE
TO THE INSIDE AND THEN IN THE MIDDLE. I WEAVE
TEXTURES AND COLORS THROUGHOUT THE WREATH
TO GIVE IT A FULL AND BALANCED FEELING."

—BARBARA APPLEBAUM

THE DESIGNER CREATED A QUIET AND LASTING BEAUTY WITH THIS DRIED WREATH BY NESTLING A VARIETY OF PASTEL FLOWERS AMIDST DELICATE GREEN FERNS.

MAKE A BASE by covering a wire frame with scraps of artemisia held tightly in place with monofilament. Fashion small bunches of fern, artemisia, baby's breath, and statice and secure them onto the base with monofilament. Glue on the dried flowers: hydrangea, globe amaranth, larkspur, pearly everlasting, carnations, and cockscomb.

"I USUALLY START OUT WITH A SPECIAL FEELING AND AN IDEA OF WHAT I WANT TO CREATE FOR EACH WREATH, BUT I DON'T DRAW OUT THE DESIGN FIRST. I GATHER THE FLOWERS I WISH TO WORK WITH AND PLACE THEM ON OR IN THE WREATH TO WORK A DESIGN.

I DON'T GLUE UNTIL I'M POSITIVE THAT THIS IS THE LOOK I WANT. SOMETIMES I'LL LEAVE THE WREATH UNGLUED UNTIL THE NEXT DAY OR A FEW HOURS LATER TO GIVE MY DESIGN A DIFFERENT PERSPECTIVE. IF I STILL LIKE IT—I GLUE. IF NOT, I'LL PLAY WITH IT UNTIL IT MATCHES WHAT MY INITIAL IDEA WAS."

—BARBARA APPLEBAUM

TANSY, ADMIRED FOR
CENTURIES FOR ITS
PINELIKE SCENT AND
PEPPERY-TASTING
LEAVES, ADDS DELICATE
COLOR AND SHAPE TO
THIS SIMPLE WREATH.

START WITH a 12-inch
(30 cm.) Spanish moss-
covered base. Wrap
green velvet ribbon
around it to form an
elegant criss-cross pat-
tern. Fashion a gener-
ous bow and wire it to
the base. Then, glue on
bunches of dried tansy
around the bow, and
scatter a few herbs ran-
domly around the rest
of the wreath. To com-
plete the focal point,
glue on some spiky
green leaves.

"ACCORDING TO WHAT TYPE OF FLOWERS I'M WORKING WITH, I DESIGN AS I GO.
SOMETIMES I GET A LINE DEVELOPING, AND I REALIZE IT'S NOT RIGHT. SO I STOP,
TAKE THE FLOWERS OUT AND REDO IT. YOU'LL KNOW WHEN YOU'VE LOST THE LINE
THAT'S MAKING YOUR WREATH VISUALLY INTERESTING OR WELL BALANCED."

—TOMMY WALLEN

THIS UNUSUAL WREATH BOLDLY CAPTURES YOUR ATTENTION IN THE SAME WAY THAT A PEACOCK SHOWS OFF ITS VIBRANT, SHIMMERING COLORS.

Weave a tapestry ribbon through a grapevine wreath, securing it with glue. Glue on a little wild clematis. Next, glue on the dried burgundy and gold cockscomb. Wire on birds' nests and use glue to keep them at the proper angles. Glue on a little down from the feathers to hide the wire in the nests. Make bundles with dried santolina flowers, pastel yarrow, and nigella pods, holding them together with floral tape. Then glue the bundles into place. Insert peacock and other feathers into the base. Lastly, glue on glycerin-preserved magnolia leaves.

"It's important to use the whole flower or foliage. If a part of a flower falls off when you are attaching it to the wreath, glue it back on."

—Josena Aiello McCaig

Start with a 16-inch (41 cm.) grapevine wreath. Glue on dried grasses in a crescent shape near the base of the wreath, weaving them into the nooks and crannies of the vine. Cut the silk sunflower stems to four to five inches (10 cm. - 13 cm.) long and poke them into the base. Use hot glue to hold the flowers in place. Make a bow with green velvet ribbon and secure it to the base with wire.

THIS STUNNING WREATH IS GENEROUS WITH ITS SIZE AND WITH THE SERVING
OF FRUITS AND VEGETABLES NESTLED ON A COOL-LOOKING BOWER OF GREENERY.

YOU'LL BE PICKING all the materials into a 24-inch (61 cm.) straw base (leave the plastic wrap on). Unfurl one 8-foot garland of artificial ivy, and pick it into the inside of the base first, then attach it to cover the front and outer sides. This method will give the wreath its full, green appearance. Fashion a very full bow from cranberry velvet ribbon and attach it to the base with picks. You'll need to secure the streamers, too. (The designer purchased one roll of #40 ribbon.) Pick in the fruits, flowers, vegetables, and pods in this order, making sure to work in a circular motion around the whole wreath: silk hydrangea (break up one large flower so you'll have smaller blossoms to work with), artificial apples, dried artichokes, halved pomegranates, plums, miniature apples, latex-covered grapes and berries, artificial heather, pods and cones, dried red eucalyptus, hydrangea leaves, artificial coleus and galax leaves, and pepperberries. Lastly, take the rest of the ribbon and split it into two narrower streamers and weave them through the foliage, using picks to secure.

THIS EXQUISITE FRESH
WREATH CONJURES UP
THE ROMANCE AND
BEAUTY OF AN OUTDOOR
WEDDING ON A SUNNY,
SPRING DAY.

INSERT ALL THE FRESH
flowers into a 20-inch
(51 cm.) oasis base,
being sure to gener-
ously cover the base.
The designer used
yellow roses, hydrangea,
lamb's ears, alstroeme-
ria, button flowers,
yarrow, and ivy.

"IF YOU'RE MAKING
EDIBLE WREATHS OR
WREATHS WITH FRESH
FLOWERS, THE OASIS
BASES ARE REALLY
FANTASTIC! THEY HOLD
THE MATERIALS WELL
AND KEEP THEM FRESH
FOR QUITE A WHILE."
—**NORA BLOSE**

THIS HANDSOME
HOLIDAY WREATH
USHERS IN THE SEASON
WITH VIBRANT REDS
AND GREENS AND
HO-HO-HO GOLDS.

START WITH A 24-inch
(61 cm.) silk evergreen
base. Glue on artificial
pomegranates. Then
glue on other materials:
gilded Queen Anne's
lace, dried lotus pods,
and deer moss. Wire
on an ample bow and
drape the long stream-
ers in and around the
other items. Lastly, glue
on several curly willow
tips fanning out from
behind the bow.

SHED

THIS ATTRACTIVE, WOODSY WREATH LOOKS LIKE IT GREW ON THIS SHED, BUT IT WOULD LOOK EQUALLY AT HOME ON A BACK PORCH OR SUN ROOM. HALF THE FUN IS WALKING IN THE WOODS TO GATHER THE MATERIALS.

REMOVE the plastic wrap from a straw wreath base. Sparingly cover the wreath with Spanish moss, securing the moss with greening pins. Glue on gray and green mosses. Wrap philodendron sheaths like ribbon around the right side of the wreath. Glue on dried ferns, lichen, other moss, acorns, and twigs. Glue on bark with fungus, fresh galax leaves, dried ferns, and leaves. Add other souvenirs from your own walk in the woods.

"The most beautiful arrangements of dried materials I have ever seen are in fields and along roadsides as they dry naturally at the end of summer."

—Cathy Barnhardt

BIRD

T HIS ARTIFICIAL HOLIDAY WREATH IN TRADITIONAL RED AND GREEN IS GIVEN AN NONTRADITIONAL PLACE OF HONOR ON A FEATHERED FRIEND'S FRONT DOOR.

START WITH A 22-inch (55.9 cm.) artificial evergreen wreath (weatherproof like a bird). Wire the pine cones together in clusters of three and wire them evenly spaced to the wreath base. Wire on grape clusters between the pine cone clusters. Make five red raffia bows and wire them to the base near the grapes. Attach Virginia creeper to floral picks and wire them to the base. For that wintery look, glue on the frosted branches.

DECK

Everything about this sunflower wreath reminded us of the outdoors, so we couldn't resist giving it a place of honor on a sunny deck (along with J.D., the beloved family dog).

Fill the watering can with artificial sunflowers, daisies, and other summer varieties, using a piece of floral foam in the can to hold the stems in place. Attach the can to a loosely woven grapevine wreath by wiring the handle to the base. To further secure it, you can poke holes in the bottom of the can, run wire through, and then wrap the wires around the wreath base. Make a bow using crepe paper or burlap ribbon and tie it onto the wreath.

"All flowers fall into four categories; round, such as a carnation or rose; form, such as a lily, orchid, or tulip; line, such as a cattail or Liatris; and filler, such as baby's breath or German statice. To avoid winding up with a boring wreath, use combinations of differently shaped flowers."

—Julianne Bronder

DESIGNER
CREDITS

The wreaths featured in this book represent the hard work, creativity, and cooperative spirit of more than a dozen designers. We thank them very, very much for their time and talent.

BARBARA APPLEBAUM and her husband, Lewis, operate Brush Creek Gardens in Fairview, North Carolina, where they grow 200 varieties of organic herbs and flowers. Barbara dries these items and markets them as raw materials and in the form of distinctive custom-made floral wreaths and arrangements. (Pages 56, 62, 70, 82, 98, 126, 130, and 138.)

CATHY BARNHARDT heads the floral department at Biltmore House and is responsible for designing many and overseeing all the floral displays in the largest private home in America. She also teaches workshops in floral design. (Pages 86, 104, and 106.)

NORA BLOSE and MICHELLE KOEPKE WEST work on many floral projects together. Nora is an herbalist from Candler, North Carolina, with a design studio called Nora's Follies. Michelle operates an in-home boutique called Floral Designs by Michelle, in Swannanoa, North Carolina, where she designs for homes, offices and weddings. (Pages 47, 67, 108, 109, 112, 117, and 141.)

JULIANNE BRONDER creates unique designs with silk flowers and natural materials. With 15 years' experience in the floral industry, Julianne also works as a floral design instructor, an interior design consultant, and a photographic stylist. (Cover, and pages 32, 37, 48, 50, 58, 69, 73, 81, 90, 97, 122, 124, and 140.)

FRED TYSON GAYLOR is a product designer for Hanford's, a wholesale holiday accessory company in Charlotte, North Carolina, and has a keen sense of current trends in the gift and accessory industry both in the U.S. and abroad. (Pages 33, 38, 64, 80, 93, 95, 116, 120, 121, and 125.)

CYNTHIA GILLOOLY and JAMIE MCCABE enjoy designing with innovative and natural materials. Cynthia owns The Golden Cricket, a floral design studio in Asheville, North Carolina, where she also teaches classes in floral design. (Pages 60, 88, and 99.) Jamie designs with her in the shop. Together they have more than 25 years of experience in all areas of floral arrangements. (Pages 42, 57, 75, 94, 110, 115, and 136.)

JEANNETTE HAFNER grows most of the flowers she uses in her floral creations in Orange, Connecticut. She teaches classes on dried flower designs and drying techniques. Her designs spring from a lifelong love of gardening and botanical painting. (Pages 51, 59, 65, 66, 76, 79, 92, 119, 128, and 132.)

JOSENA AIELLO MCCAIG was formerly on the floral display staff at Biltmore House, where she learned to love working on a large scale. She now operates her own floral design studio called "Some Parlor Ivy," in Asheville, North Carolina. (Pages 28, 36, 41, 45, 61, 71, and 84.)

LUCK MCELREATH has been a floral designer for ten years, and together with her husband, Lewis, operates the Flower Gallery. Her specialty is oriental designs, and she enjoys finding creative ways to make her floral arrangements reflect the personality of the customer. (Pages 34, 39, 83, and 135.)

NICOLE VICTORIA is nationally known for her designs of Victorian-era crafts, gifts, and lifestyle accessories. She lives in Asheville, North Carolina. (Pages 44, 102, and 113.)

TOMMY WALLEN specializes in innovative wedding and party floral displays and his work has won numerous blue ribbons and awards. He has worked at Gudger's Flowers in Asheville, North Carolina for the past four years. (Pages 31, 49, 53, 54, 96, 100, and 133.)

Also thanks to JANE DICUS (page 101), JANET FRYE (page 129), KIT MECKLEY (page 30), and to the following people who generously opened their homes to us: BARBARA and LEWIS APPLEBAUM, ANN BATCHELDER and HENRI KIEFFER, DEBORAH and MICHAEL BUCK, VIRGINIA and THOMAS HONEA, JULIE and BRUCE HOWERTON, EVELYN and FRANK MORRISON, ROB PULLEN, GAIL and TEDD SMITH, ELIZABETH SIMS (who opened the enormous doors of Biltmore House), and a special thanks to JUDY LALLY, who helped open the doors to several beautiful, although smaller, homes featured in this book.

INDEX